Elements of Style for Screenwriters

by Paul Argentini

lone eagle™

Los Angeles, CA

Elements of Style for Screenwriters
© Copyright 1998 by Paul M. Argentini. All rights reserved.

LONE EAGLE PUBLISHING CO., LLC™
2337 Roscomare Road, Suite Nine
Los Angeles, CA 90077-1851
Phone: 800-FILMBKS • Toll Free Fax: 888-FILMBKS
www.loneeagle.com & www.eaglei.com

Printed in the United States of America

Cover design by Blake Busby
Book design by Carla Green
Edited by Janna Wong Healy

Library of Congress Cataloging-in-Publication Data

Argentini, Paul
    Elements of style for screenwriters / by Paul Argentini.
        p.   cm.
    ISBN 1-58065-003-1
        1. Motion picture authorship.   2. Television authorship.
I. Title.
PN1996.A73   1998
808.2'3--dc21   98-22446
                                                    CIP

. . . But the artist appeals to that part of our being which is not dependent on wisdom: to that in us which is a gift and not an acquisition—and, therefore, more permanently enduring. He speaks to our capacity for delight and wonder, to the sense of mystery surrounding our lives; to our sense of pity, and beauty, and pain; to the latent feeling of fellowship with all creation—and to the subtle but invincible conviction of solidarity that knits together the loneliness of innumerable hearts, to the solidarity in dreams, in joy, in sorrow in aspirations, in illusions, in hopes, in fear, which binds men to each other, which binds together all humanity—the dead to the living and the living to the unborn.

—Joseph Conrad
1897

Excerpted from *The Children of the Sea: A Tale of the Forecastle*, by Joseph Conrad, Doubleday, New York, NY, 1942.

To Lisa and Mona

Also by Paul Argentini:

Coauthor
MUSICALS! Directing School and Community Theatre

One-Act Plays
No Gas For Nick
Pearl Seed

CONTENTS

INDEX OF SCREENWRITING ELEMENTS

INDEX OF PLAYWRITING ELEMENTS

PREFACE

This compilation was started some years ago, shortly after I was captivated by the screenwriting process. Anxious to start creating, I found that the format kept getting in the way of my writing. The first guidebook I bought (for $2.00) was a 25-page monograph published by the Writers Guild of America, East, Inc.[1] Not counting illustrations, the actual number of instructional pages on screenwriting format came to about three, with another three pages for camera terms. Yet, a note in the addendum read: "It is not unusual to see a modern screenplay with virtually no camera angles at all, . . ." Included was a very short sample of a screenplay page, with slug lines, direction and dialogue. It ended with the note, "Directors will bless you for leaving most of the shots to them." Now that admonition would read: "Directors will hate and resent you if you don't!"

Today, books are readily available on formatting—some 200 pages long! Most are quite complete, but I found them cumbersome—in style and size. For one thing, they offer many sample pages, using both right and wrong examples, but the information contained in them jumbled in my brain and I couldn't remember one rule from another. I checked into a few computer screenwriting software programs, only to find my unorganized mind could neither understand nor master them. I spent a lot of time hunting the answers to such questions as, "What's the format for this? For that? For this and that?"

[1]Coopersmith, Jerome. *Professional Writer's Teleplay/Screenplay Format,* New York, NY: Writers Guild of America, East, Inc., 1970, Rev. Ed. 1983, pp. 25.

I began writing down the correct process for those points I used the most or were difficult to recall. Slowly, I added to my personal guide until it was fairly comprehensive. Developing macros, I came up with my own screenwriting program. Using my own guide as an adjunct, which I kept at my computer keyboard, it took seconds to hunt up a forgotten format element. I would ask myself, "How do I do that close-up thing?" then flip the pages and "Insert" would pop up before me, complete with protocol.

Would this guide be of use to an experienced screenwriter who owned mega-millibyte writing programs? True, he'd have all the elements on his computer program. But, say the writer didn't know what he was looking for—how could the answer be found? He wouldn't have that problem with a guidebook. Would it be of use to a novice screenwriter? If he didn't know the lingo, he couldn't understand the language and thus, he couldn't produce a professional piece of work.

This is meant to be a self-teaching sourcebook. Beginners should read *Elements of Style for Screenwriters* from cover to cover in order to have an idea about formatting and what is involved. Then follow the suggested "Format Study Guide" which follows for familiarization and to get a feeling of what formatting a screenplay is about. Then go through the elements one more time, studying each one to understand its use. Finally, read a few professionally-written screenplays.

And what about the writer who doesn't have a screenwriting program and has to hunt around for answers to format questions? I remember my own first sorry mess. Therefore, comfort and confidence will be gained by having this book next to your keyboard.

From my experience, I gleaned more from reading screenplays than from filtering through format books. One soon gets the idea of which elements are cast in stone and which are more flexible. For example, one doesn't fool around with slug lines. On the other hand, the narrative in direction allows for individual creativity in describing an action scene or a compelling moment. (After all, even Beethoven broke the rules of classical music composition when he said content would set form, rather than the other way around.) But, before one gets too far afield, bear in mind that a chess board cannot be set up any which way. (What a hell of a game that would be!) If I may, temper your freedom not with thoughts of whimsical self-indulgence, but with thoughts of perfection.

One major factor I learned about the screenplay format is that no element is arbitrary—there is a reason for every one. Thus, the rationale for the element is your clue to the format.

I emphasize: Do not restrict your use of any element to the example given. In its use, be brave when you must, be creative always. I found no book offering rationale for the screenwriting page as I do, which is the foundation for the screenwriting format. None of the format books offered a complete, easy-to-find alphabetical listing of formats, guides and hints, right along with protocol. None gave insight into a macro that will allow a screenwriter to generate an easy-to-use screenwriting program.

"Accepted industry *standard* format" is an amorphous ideal. Studios and production companies each has its preferred style. Also, variations include all the versions a script must go through before it becomes a film. Variables—major or minor—exist. Not right, not wrong—just "different." One format melds into another. As if to prove this point, the format now is to double space between scenes, a technique used previously only to condense a script. A triple space before a slug line was the "old" protocol.

There will be some repetitious information on these pages. But, there are no wrong examples to remember. *The Elements of Style for Screenwriters* was not written to teach screenwriting or to give you an insight into the dramatic art, although it might come close and I beg your forgiveness. It will, however, help you learn, understand and be able to use the elements necessary to put a screenplay on paper. It will be like going to a smorgasbord: the fun at a feast is variety, variety, variety! And so it is for a screenplay. Don't try something just to try it or to show that you're a professional. Use the armada of elements to your advantage and choose the one that is the best device to bring to a reality the clearest vision of your idea. Visual—that's what movies are all about.

If you were a development executive, which would you prefer: A mediocre screenplay that is beautifully formatted or an exceptional screenplay that is not formatted so expertly? Some say, once you understand the screenwriting format, you shouldn't let it bog you down.

But, by the same token, a photographer who doesn't understand the mechanics of his own camera can't concentrate on the process of taking the pictures. The same rule applies to screenwriting: Understand the mechanics of screenwriting but don't let them get in the way of your art. I hope this guide will help you get over the formatting hurdle.

Final notes: When you go to a movie or watch a TV drama, do it with a sheet of paper and a pencil. Make a mark every time the shot on the screen changes. To generate this little drama, write down how many marks you think you'll make before the show begins. Look at your sheet when the show is over. An enormous surprise is in store for you.

Now, note that every one of those marks has something to do with *The Elements of Style for Screenwriters*.

—PMA
Great Barrington, Massachusetts
1998

FORMAT STUDY GUIDE

For those unfamiliar with screenplay formatting, this suggested format study guide is designed to get the reader "up to speed" as quickly as possible. After going through the entire text from cover-to-cover, re-read the definitions for the elements listed below in the following suggested order.

BOOK 1

SCREENWRITING

SAMPLE SCREENPLAY

"FUNNY YOU SHOULD ASK"

Written by

Throckmorton T. Throckmorton

T. T. THROCKMORTON
555 Fifth Avenue
Fiveville, FL 33516
Tel: 813.555-1212
Fax: 813.555-1234

"FUNNY YOU SHOULD ASK"

FADE IN:

EXT. NEW YORK SKYLINE - DAY - ESTABLISHING - STOCK (2000)

INT. VET'S EXAMINING ROOM - DAY

Veterinarian THROCKMORTON T. THROCKMORTON wearing a
white examining jacket is spraying disinfectant on the
examining table and polishing it with a cloth when
LUDVINNIA enters holding a shoe box. He wipes the smile
from his face when he sees she is obviously quite sad
and concerned.

                        LUDVINNIA
                  (half-smiling)
            Dr. Throckmorton, I called. I'm
            Ludvinnia.

                    THROCKMORTON
            How we doing?
                  (a beat)

He sprays and polishes for just a bit, then turns to
her.

                    THROCKMORTON
                  (continuing)
            What have we here?
                  (points to the shoe box)

THE SHOE BOX

It's a scruffy-looking shoebox for aerobic sneaks held
together with a rubber band.

BACK TO SCENE

                        LUDVINNIA
            I'm doing fine, but I'm very worried
            about my dear pet.

2.

                    THROCKMORTON
              (nods - solicitously)
         Yes, of course. Shall we have a
         look?

Ludvinnia puts the box on the examining table. She
sees a box of tissues on the counter, and helps her-
self. She dries her eyes.

Throckmorton makes a move to remove the rubber band,
but Ludvinnia holds up a hand to stop him. She pets
the box, then yanks off the rubber band. She looks
hard into the vet's eyes as she removes the top of the
box.

                    THROCKMORTON
              (gasps - covers his eyes)
         It's a parakeet!

INSERT - PARAKEET IN BOX

that is lying very still on its side.

BACK TO SCENE

                    THROCKMORTON
              (continuing)
         I'm sorry to tell you, Ma'am, but
         your parakeet looks . . . dead, I
         mean, really kaput.

Ludvinnia grabs Throckmorton by his lapels, and shakes
him.

LUDVINNIA'S POV - THROCKMORTON

The vet's face, eyes opened wide, draws near, then
moves away doing this several times.

                    LUDVINNIA (O.S.)
              (a beat; then wildly)
         That can't be!

BACK TO SCENE

                    LUDVINNIA
        I loved that pet like I was a
        bird!

                    THROCKMORTON
                (smoothing his jacket)
        No question, you did.

                    LUDVINNIA
        Understand you! He's got to be
        okay or I'll be guilt-ridden the
        rest of my life! I forgot to feed
        him when I got up this morning
        only to find him like this later.
        Sir! He mustn't be kaput!

                    THROCKMORTON
        You want confirmation? Okay.

He opens the door and makes twitching sounds to call a
cat.

TABBY enters the examining room. Throckmorton taps the
top of the examining table.

SERIES OF SHOTS

A) Tabby jumps atop the table

B) Tabby walks around the shoe box

C) Tabby sniffs the parakeet

D) Tabby hops off the table and exits

END SERIES OF SHOTS

Throckmorton throws his hands in the air.

                    THROCKMORTON
            That confirms it, Ludvinnia. Your
            parakeet is gone. Sorry.

                    LUDVINNIA
                (jutting her chin)
            I was hoping you wouldn't say
            that. I still have payments to
            make on him. What do I owe you?

4.

>   THROCKMORTON
> I'm sure you understand,
> Ludvinnia, what with the exorbitant
> malpractice insurance costs . . .

Ludvinnia crosses her arms, raises an eyebrow and
gives him a hard, penetrating stare.

>   THROCKMORTON
>   (continuing; a beat)
> . . . rising, taxes going up and
> so on. My fee is $400.00

>   LUDVINNIA
> Would you be kind enough to itemize
> that for me without the violin mu-
> sic?

>   THROCKMORTON
> Certainly. It's $30.00 for the of-
> fice visit, and $370.00 for the
> cat scan.

FADE OUT.

T H E   E N D

T.T. THROCKMORTON
555 Fifth Avenue
Fiveville, FL 33516
Tel: 813.555-1212
Fax: 813.555-1234

SAMPLE SCREENPLAY, ANNOTATED

"FUNNY YOU SHOULD ASK"

Written by

Throckmorton T. Throckmorton

T. T. THROCKMORTON
555 Fifth Avenue
Fiveville, FL 33516
Tel: 813.555-1212
Fax: 813.555-1234

title down six spaces -   "FUNNY YOU SHOULD ASK"

double space
FADE IN:
double space to
EXT. NEW YORK SKYLINE - DAY - EST. - opening slug line OCK (2000)
double space to
INT. VET'S EXAMINING ROOM - DAY   - master slug line
double space to
Veterinarian THROCKMORTON T. THROCKMORTON wearing a
white examining jacket is sprayin - direction ectant on the
examining table and polishing it with a cloth when
LUDVINNIA - capitalize names of characters first time only   pes the smile
from his face when he sees she is obviously quite sad
and concerned.

                    character name -   LUDVINNIA
        parenthetical dialogue -   (half-smiling)
                    Dr. Throckmorton, I called. I'm
                    Ludvinnia.

                        THROCKMORTON
                    How we doing?
                        (a beat)

He sprays and polishes for just a bit, then turns to
her.   - direction interrupts his speech

                        THROCKMORTON
        his speech continues -   (continuing)
                    What have we here?
                parenthetical -   (points to the shoe box)

THE SHOE BOX - subsidiary slug line

It's a scruffy-looking shoebox for aerobic sneaks held
together with a rubber band.   - description of slug line

BACK TO SCENE - end the slug line to get back to the original shot

                        LUDVINNIA
                    I'm doing fine, but I'm very worried
                    about my dear pet.

use plain Arabic numbers -   2.

THROCKMORTON

dual parenthetical - (nods - solicitously)
Yes, of course. Shall we have a
look?

Ludvinnia puts the box on the examining table. She
sees a box of tissues on the counter, and helps her-
self. She dries her eyes.

Throckmorton makes a move to remove the rubber band,
but Ludvinnia holds up a hand to stop him. She pets
the box, then yanks off the rubber band. She looks
hard into the vet's eyes as she removes the top of the
box.

THROCKMORTON

dual parenthetical - (gasps - covers his eyes)
It's a parakeet!

double space to Insert element
INSERT - PARAKEET IN BOX

that is lying very still on its side. - describe what we're
looking at

BACK TO SCENE - end the element

THROCKMORTON

(continuing)   - dialogue continues after direction
I'm sorry to tell you, Ma'am, but
your parakeet looks . . . dead, I
mean, really kaput.

Ludvinnia grabs Throckmorton by his lapels, and shakes
him.

LUDVINNIA'S POV - THROCKMORTON   - POV slug line

The vet's face, eyes opened wide, -draws near, then
moves away doing this several times. - what's being seen

we're looking at him and hearing her -   LUDVINNIA (O.S.)
(a beat; then wildly)   - dual parenthetical
That can't be!   with beat and
semicolon

BACK TO SCENE - end the element

page number -   3.

(continuing) not needed here—   LUDVINNIA
LUDVINNIA (O.S.)   I loved that pet like I was a bird!
and LUDVINNIA
are separate elements

                    THROCKMORTON
               (smoothing his jacket)
          No question, you did.

                    LUDVINNIA
          Understand you! He's got to be okay
          or I'll be guilt-ridden the rest of
          my life! I forgot to feed him when
          I got up this morning only to find
          him like this later. Sir! He
          mustn't be kaput!

                    THROCKMORTON
          You want confirmation? Okay.

He opens the door and makes twitching sounds to call a
cat.

TABBY enters the examining room. Throckmorton taps the
top of the examining table.
double space to element
SERIES OF SHOTS

A)   Tabby jumps atop the table

B)   Tabby walks around the shoe box

C)   Tabby sniffs the parakeet

D)   Tabby hops off the table and exits

END SERIES OF SHOTS - end the element

Throckmorton throws his hands in the air.

                    THROCKMORTON
          That confirms it, Ludvinnia. Your
          parakeet is gone. Sorry.

                    LUDVINNIA
               (jutting her chin)
          I was hoping you wouldn't say
          that. I still have payments to
          make on him. What do I owe you?

page number -   4.

                    THROCKMORTON
          I'm sure you understand, Ludvinnia,
          what with the exorbitant malprac-
          tice insurance costs . . .

Ludvinnia crosses her arms, raises an eyebrow and gives
him a hard, penetrating stare.

                    THROCKMORTON
                (continuing; a beat)   - semicolon for this
ellipsis marks -   . . . rising, taxes going up dual parenthetical
show speech   on. My fee is $400.00
goes right on

                    LUDVINNIA
          Would you be kind enough to itemize
          that for me without the violin mu-
          sic?

                    THROCKMORTON
          Certainly. It's $30.00 for the of-
          fice visit, and $370.00 for the cat
          scan.

               one and only time to use this -   FADE OUT.

six spaces

          in caps -   T H E   E N D

This is the third source address put in the script -   T.T. THROCKMORTON
                                                       555 Fifth Avenue
                                                       Fiveville, FL 33516
                                                       Tel: 813.555-1212
                                                       Fax: 813.555-1234

SCREENWRITING ELEMENTS

A   ## ACTS

The technical construction of a dramatic work. Reference may be made to "acts" in a screenplay.

In theater, an act is a quantitative unit made up of beats, segments, French scenes and scenes that make up a play. At one time, the norm was three acts; the format today for a full-length play is two acts, although dinner theater still prefers three acts with two intermissions. And there are exceptions: Shakespeare's *Hamlet* contains five acts.

In current dramatic structure, the two-act play usually is written in three acts; the same is true of the screenplay. (A full-length dramatic screenplay would have a beginning, middle and end. Hence, three "acts.")

The three acts are broken down as follows:

• The beginning usually is expository, or relates to what happened just before the action begins.

• The middle is where the dramatist throws more coals onto the fire to increase tension and suspense. ("Second-act problems" are a common occurrence.)

• In the final act, the action is brought to the highest possible dramatic height. Then, the denouement occurs, which ends the drama, leaving everyone satisfied and content.

AD LIB

A

Without restraint and, in particular, to spontaneous, improvised speech or patter.

It is a direction and is usually written in all capital letters. Instead of the author writing dialogue for an individual or for, say, 20 couples in the background at a cocktail party, the actors are at liberty to ad lib—invent or create their own appropriate patter, laughter, smiles, scowls, greetings or looks to convey the impression of reality. Usually, the speeches are not distinct unless the intent is to heighten the drama. In such a case, the author must qualify in the script the tenor of the ad libs. For example, an angry crowd after the hero would ad lib exclamations such as, "Hang 'im!" or "Tar and feathers!"

In the script, ad lib would be found, as follows:

```
AD LIB cocktail party chatter.
```

A ADDRESS

Also called "Source Address," this is found on the TITLE PAGE—the very first page of the script after the hard cover.

The author's name, address, and phone number should be typed in the lower right-hand corner, single-spaced, on separate lines. It is your choice whether to include your fax number and e—mail address. In place of the author's information can be typed the owner of the script or the author's representative.

Surprisingly, many scripts are sent without the Source Address. (Confusion may have arisen long ago, when it was considered gauche to enclose a self-addressed, stamped envelope [SASE] with the script submission, because screenplays were never returned anyway. But then, how did an interested party know who to contact and where?) Modesty is a virtue but sending out an anonymous script is ridiculous. Always enclosed a SASE.

There are two other locations where the author may wish to put the source address, in case the title page should become lost:

• You may wish to place it on the last page of the script, close to the bottom of the page, on the right. Or,

• You may select a page in the middle of the script (say, page 50) and insert it vertically, along the left-hand edge of the page between the fastener holes.

AGENT

Also known as a literary agent, literary representative or author's representative, this person acts for you in marketing what you create as a writer.

The agent aids the writer because he allows the author to concentrate on writing rather than selling his work; his presence cuts down on office procedures involving cover letters, mailings, recording keeping; and more often than not, he'll get more money for the property than if the author were to sell it himself. For this service, he receives a commission based on a percentage of the sale. The agent negotiates the financial details involving all the rights to the written property. Agents of all types are found across the country, but generally, agents dealing in the film and television industries are located on the West Coast while those dealing in publishing, theater and television are located in New York City.

Agents generally specialize in a particular general field, e.g., films, books, television, or they may specialize even further, e.g., feature films or movies of the week; trade or children's books; TV sitcoms or dramatic series. Specialization is fostered because many sales come through personal acquaintance or contacts built up over the years.

Today, an agent is almost mandatory when selling a property. An agent is not a film doctor; he may not suggest revisions or cuts. Rather, he acts as the primary filter of a writer's effort, supposedly keeping lower-quality scripts out of the marketplace. Many film companies and producers will not accept submissions unless they come through an agent.

Engaging an agent—or selling your own script—will be like pushing a boulder up a very steep mountain, but, take heart! The better your screenplay, the smaller the boulder.

A AUTHOR'S SCRIPT

Also known as the "selling script," it is the version in which the sole, unabashed, blatant purpose is to seduce the reader into thinking it will make a movie. This version sells the story.

The author's script is free of all technical or production impedimenta, such as numbered scenes, numbered inserts and (especially) camera angles. The author's script is properly formatted and reads quickly and easily. However, allowances are made in formatting so the author can clearly describe what he sees in his mind's eye vs. what he must put down on paper to make that vision as clear as possible.

Screenwriting is an art. As such, it is one of the reasons screenplay formatting often goes awry. Creativity and individuality play a part in generating a unique script. One author may take one paragraph to describe an action scene. Another may use ten lines. There is no right or wrong here. The test is clarity.

BACK TO SCENE

A slug line, written in the directions and typed in all capital letters, flush with the left-hand margin.

During a scene, there may be a break to another short scene (in effect, a scene within a scene, i.e., sending the action to the base runner on first base then returning to the action on the baseball diamond). To indicate that you are returning to the original scene, give the slug line direction, "BACK TO SCENE." The simultaneous element (or scene within the scene) is ended, closed or stopped and indication that the element is ended is made with any of the following: "BACK TO SCENE," direction description, action or a new slug line.

Check out the use of "BACK TO SCENE" with INSERT (page 77) and POV (page 103).

Example:

```
INT. BAR - NIGHT

There is a large, mixed crowd sitting, standing.
AD LIB small talk fills the room. The COP turns to
look around.

BOOTH

THROCKMORTON reaches over to take LUDVINNIA's
hand. He slips a ring on her finger.

                    LUDVINNIA
          Where did you get the money?

BACK TO SCENE

The bartender nods his head to the Cop for his
order.
```

B BACKGROUND

Also written as b.g., this is a slug line stage direction describing the background in a scene or a background SOUND.

What is found in the background is usually subsidiary to the main action and is most often used to add to the atmosphere. If it appears in the middle of a sentence, both letters are in lower case; if the abbreviation begins a sentence, capitalize the "b."

Example:

```
In the b.g. the enemy tank CLANKS around the far
corner with its cannon firing, machine gun going.
B.g. RAT-A-TAT is heard from the machine guns.
```

BEAT

Used to indicate a brief or passing moment that usually signals reflective thought or a hesitation in the action to heighten suspense; a brief moment free of dialogue.

The beat is parenthetical (it is placed in parentheses, typed in lower case letters and used in the talent or dialogue element). A beat is as long as the director or actor feels it should be for that particular moment. Inserting a beat borders on directing, so the author must feel the moment is necessary. Such as:

```
                    THROCKMORTON
          Did I say that?
                    (beat)
          I wasn't sure . . .
```

In playwriting, the duration of a beat is defined, such as:

```
                    THROCKMORTON
      Did I say that?
                    (beat — a three-count)
      I wasn't sure . . .
```

B BINDING

The fastening of a script. All scripts must be bound with two or three round-headed brass fasteners called "Brads." Number Five (1-1/2") or Number Seven (2") are acceptable. Open the prongs and flatten them against the back script cover. Don't do anything else to them! Some script readers like to take out the fasteners and read the script with loose pages; they can't do this if you have made them tamper-proof by turning them into butterfly wings or the like. Therefore, do not put tape over the ends of the fasteners; do not fold or bend the ends of the fasteners. Available, though not recommended, are small, metal washers with slits in them used on the back side of the screenplay to hold the fastener and keep it from tearing the paper. And, clamp-type binders or fold-over fasteners used for stage play scripts should not be used.

The prongs are an accepted industry hazard, although the post office may not appreciate scripts bound this way if you mail them in flimsy envelopes and the brads poke through.

A three-hole punch is a worthwhile investment.

BLOCKING

B

The positioning of an actor from place to place.

Blocking and movement are not the same thing and are not to be confused. Movement describes how the blocking occurs, i.e., slowly, quickly, sauntering. An actor may be blocked to stand behind a desk or walk to a window. (Blocking and Movement are not to be confused with BUSINESS.)

The author blocks a character when he places the actor in a particular spot, such as behind a desk, in a car, on a horse. This is mainly a theatrical term, but it is used by the scriptwriter to place characters, such as:

```
Blocking at the bridge table: Mary and Janice
(North and South) are seated. Molly (East) is
standing behind her chair. Eunice (West) is
standing at the bar.
```

B

BREAKING DIALOGUE

Dialogue that is interrupted. All breaking dialogue requires specific protocol involving the use of CONTINUATIONS. (See page 48).

There are two main reasons for breaking dialogue:

- The first is a break by direction. For example, if action occurs during an actor's speech, it may cause the actor to stop talking momentarily (or not) and may or may not be noticed by the actor. Call this an action interruption.

- The second is a mechanical interruption, when the dialogue reaches the end or bottom of the page. Then it "breaks" onto the next page. Make the break in a logical place, say at the end of a sentence or at a pause.

Dialogue may be broken simultaneously by direction and the end of a page.

BUSINESS

An actor's incidental actions, such as adjusting a tie, picking up a key or fishing through a purse; also refers to the narrative written and is known as direction.

These actions are not necessarily written into a script (except for characterization) and are not "set" but depend on an individual's mannerisms or acting style. Writing in business is overkill unless it is germane to the character. Also, it detracts from the story line. It engenders yawns.

When included as direction, it encompasses all aspects of the playwright's vision of the story and how it takes place; it is not how it is photographed.

C · CAMERA

The sole province of the director, although you, as author, must write what you see through the camera in your mind's eye. Your vision, as clearly as you can make it, comes first; everyone else's creativity comes after.

As an author, give camera directions at your own risk: in other words, don't use them in your script! If you feel you must, think about becoming a director. Camera angles and directions are not necessary in a selling script; they slow down the proceedings, like paying a toll on a highway. If your vision calls for a specific view and a particular camera angle, then find another way to write it. For example, do not write: "LONG SHOT on a flock of crows." A better way is to write, "In the far distance, we SEE a flock of crows." Say what you mean and trust the director to make it happen. Be a storyteller, not a cameraperson.

CAST

Refers to all characters who appear in the movie.

The author's script does not carry a cast list but it is included in the final film, either in the front credits (or titles) or in the end credit crawl. The author should not indicate where the credits are to appear in a film—unless there is a specific purpose for doing so. They can be simply indicated, "Main Titles Begin," and "Main Titles End."

A cast list usually does not include actors playing very minor roles, appearing in nonspeaking roles or as background "atmosphere."

C CHARACTER NAME

The name of the part which the actor plays in the film. It is separated by two spaces above, and always typed in all caps. It begins at the same mark, 3.5" in from the left-hand edge of the paper, no matter how long or short the character's name is.

CHARACTER NAME

The character name is never left hanging alone at the bottom of a page. Move it to the next page, where it will be attached to the dialogue. The dialogue to be spoken is directly below it, typed in its dialogue column beginning 2.5" in from the left-hand edge of the paper.

Use the same character name throughout the script. For example, if you introduce a character as COLONEL SMITH, don't change it to COLONEL halfway in. If a character has a particular role, such as artist, policeman, mention that in the description of the character when the character is first introduced.

A character name may be an occupation, such as WAITRESS or TICKET SELLER. If more than one type of the same type of character name is used, they can be numbered, e.g., SWIMMER #1, SWIMMER #2, SWIMMER #3.

CHARACTER INTRODUCTION

The first mention of a character in the script.

When this occurs, the character's name is typed in all capital letters, after which, the character's name is written in upper and lower case.

If the character's dialogue is coming from "off-screen," "off stage," or is a "voice-over," then this is so noted by using the abbreviations (O.S.) and (V.O.), typed in all capitals on the same line as the Character Name.

Example:

```
             Cathy (O.S.)
     I can't hear you! I'm in the
     shower!
```

Here the voice over would come from a mechanical device such as a cell phone, speaker, answering machine:

```
             Throckmorton (V.O.)
     Dialogue would be written here.
```

C CHARACTER'S SPEECH

The character's speech, or DIALOGUE, is written directly below the character name or PARENTHETICAL. It is single-spaced, upper and lower case and falls within the talent column. Dialogue should begin 2.5" from the left-hand edge of the page.

At the end of the speech, double-space to the next character name or direction. Double-space to the next slug line. When your character's dialogue has been interrupted by direction, indicate (continuing) as a parenthetical under the character's name. When the dialogue continues to the next page, indicate (MORE) at the end of the first page, and (CONT'D.) on the subsequent page next to the character's name. Then continue with the dialogue.

- Personal direction or action (see PARENTHETICALS, page 100);

- Off Screen/Off Stage or Voice Over qualifiers (see pages 96 and 140);

- Foreign language or accent (see page 76).

CLOSE-UP

"CLOSE-UP" and "EXTREME CLOSE-UP" are camera angles. "CLOSE SHOT" is another camera angle. These should not be used in the author's script. Instead, use "INSERT." If you absolutely must use "close-up," or "extreme close-up," spell it out in capital letters, or abbreviate it *"CU" or "ECU."*

```
EXTREME CLOSE-UP - PHOTO IN WATCH CASE
```

or:

```
ECU PHOTO IN WATCH CASE
```

C

CONTINUATION

This applies to interrupted dialogue and/or direction. In order to prepare shooting scripts, the unit production managers will usually mark all scenes that continue from one page to the next at the bottom and top of each applicable page. This is unnecessary for the writer, and takes up space. Some scriptwriting programs have this feature as an option. All writers need to do now is mark "(MORE)" at the end of any page in which dialogue is interrupted, and "(CONT'D.)" beside the character name on the following page.

                    THROCKMORTON
          Did I tell you about the horse that
          walked into a bar—

                    (MORE)

———————————————————PAGE BREAK———————————————————

                    THROCKMORTON (CONT'D.)
          —and the bartender asked him, "Why
          the long face?"

When direction is continued from one page to the next, no additional notation is necessary. If dialogue is broken mid page by direction, you may indicate (cont'd.) next to the character's next speech or (continuing) in the parenthetical.

                    THROCKMORTON
          Did I tell you about the horse that
          walked into a bar—

Ludvinnia drops the broom and dustpan in disgust.

                    THROCKMORTON
                    (continuing)
          —and the bartender asked him, "Why
          the long face?"

COPYRIGHT

The exclusive legal right to a literary, dramatic, musical or artistic work which allows the owner of the copyright in matter and form to sell, reproduce, publish or produce it. Copyright is granted for a definite period of time.

One method of protecting your work against infringement or unauthorized use is by obtaining a copyright. Due to changing regulations, write to the address below for the latest information, forms and fees.

Registrar of Copyrights
Library of Congress
Washington, D.C. 20559

The Library of Congress Public Information Office has a hotline you may wish to call: 202-707-3000. To order copyright forms, call 202-707-9100. Their website is: http://lcweb.loc.gov.

When you apply for a copyright, you will need to submit a hard (printed) copy of your work. The current filing fee is $20. Some say that "common law copyright" is good enough protection; others say if you copyright your work, it will date your script. You must decide which way you have the most to gain or lose.

The Copyright Office receives more than 600,000 applications annually. It keeps no breakdowns for stage, screen or television scripts but industry estimates are that 150,000 of them are screenplays.

See also REGISTRATION, page 109.

C COVER

The card stock front and back script covers. If you choose to put a cover on your script, use plain, colored (not white) card stock, generally 65 lb. to 110 lb. card stock. Do not put any writing on the cover. Do not cover the spine of the script. The cover is used mainly for protection. Most studios and production companies don't use covers and it is becoming more common practice by professionals not to.

CUE

A signal or warning. It comes from the Latin, *quando*, meaning "when." In screenplay terminology, it is the signal for a specific piece of business on or off stage.

A cue may be a word—such as the last word, or last several words—of an actor's speech indicating another actor's lines or that some stage business will follow. A cue found in the stage directions may be for some stage business that prompts a speech or action. For example:

```
When the phone RINGS, the actors sit.
```

C   CUT TO:

Refers to a specific and abrupt change of locale. Technically, every scene could end with a "CUT TO:" All transitions are assumed to be cuts, so the author does not have to indicate them in the script. Use it sparingly and with discretion, but use it if you must, particularly when there is a dramatic shift in locale, say from the desert to a waterfall. There are times when a scene calls for a different technical ending. In such a case, the author may use "DISSOLVE TO:" or "MATCH CUT TO:"

Cuts may end a page. Cuts may not be used to begin a page. "DISSOLVE TO:" ends a scene. It is also used for dramatic effect, indicating the scene gradually fades away. "MATCH CUT TO:" uses the same object in two or more succeeding shots, scenes or sequences, as a form of shorthand to show the passage of time or distance.

These are written in capital letters followed by a colon, in the transitional camera column, 6-1/2" from the left-hand edge of the page.

DASH

When a character's speech is interrupted—or broken—it is indicated by a dash, which is typed with two hyphens. The dash should not be used instead of dots for ellipsis marks. (See ELLIPSIS MARKS, page 65.)

D ## DATE

Scene headings (slug lines) may include the date, season, time of day.

The date is placed in the slug line, in parentheses. Where the date appears in the slug line depends on whether it modifies a particular location for a particular shot, or whether is describes the period of the entire film. For example:

```
EXT. DENVER, COLORADO (1863) - DAY
```

If the date is Historical Time, then in the first primary slug line, it is typed, in parentheses, in capitals, flush with the right-hand column. For example:

```
EXT. VALLEY FORGE - DAY              (WINTER 1776)
```

At one time the title page used to contain date information, including draft, date and number of the draft. This practice is now obsolete. The date is also used on revised pages of a shooting script, which does not apply to the author's script.

A date (year) is required in any copyright notice.

DIALOGUE

D

The words spoken by a character—to himself or to someone else.

Dialogue is restricted to the center dialogue or talent column. It is written in upper and lower case letters and is single-spaced. Double-space from the last line of dialogue to the next line of type.

>   THROCKMORTON
>   Throckmorton, the character's
>   name, is the cue for dialogue.
>   What he says goes directly
>   under his name in the dialogue
>   column, like this.

No other character name, direction or dialogue may be included; these must be given their own specific elements. For instance, if Ludvinnia interrupts his speech by dropping a tray, it would be written as a separate direction, like this:

Ludvinnia enters, sees Throckmorton, and drops a tray of dishes.

>   THROCKMORTON
>   (continuing)
>   He would go on with his
>   dialogue as written.

continued on next page

D

DIALOGUE *continued from previous page*

Dialogue may have several elements:

- The character name (who is going to speak the words).

- Qualifiers, such as (V.O.) and (O.S.).

- The speech (words to be said).

- The parentheticals (personal direction or action—the manner or how the words will be said).

Abbreviate titles, such as Ms., Mrs., Ms., Dr., Capt.

If the screenwriter wants to describe a brief *action*, such as, "looks at his wristwatch" or "glances at the burning fuse," it is put directly under the character's name and indented from the left dialogue margin. It is single-spaced and put in parentheses, typed in all lower case letters, as follows:

```
                    FRED
               (whistles)
          Somebody!
```

If the parenthetical notation needs more than one line, it maintains the same left-hand margin. Such as:

```
                 THROCKMORTON
              (picks up the knife and the
              tomahawk)
          Do not threaten me!
```

Anything longer than two lines is written as a direction before the character's name; or, it is written during or after the dialogue.

D

The second type of parenthetical direction is when the author wants the character to speak a line in a particular manner, such as "angrily," "mockingly" or "indignantly." This is known as "personal direction." Be careful. The red flag says, "Directing." Directors dislike personal direction because actors usually are loathe to discard their first readings and often do not experiment with other possibilities. Good writing should dictate the mood of the speech. And, personal direction can be better done indirectly, via stage directions, by an action or a piece of business. Screenwriter Don Petersen relates the time Paul Newman noted one of his parentheticals, and asked Don to show him how someone would "smile laconically." If you feel you should give the character personal direction, write it as straight direction and perhaps the director won't notice. For example:

```
                    THROCKMORTON
          I can't do that, no matter what you
          say!
```

He smirks, glances at the gun. Cheek twitching, he stares into the man's eyes. His hand trembles, then it reaches for the weapon.

D DIRECTION

The element that carries the author's vision, including the description of the setting, action, characters, atmosphere, props or whatever else the author imagines to be seen and heard on the screen. If it "directs" anything, it is the narrative.

It is called "direction," because before sound movies, this was reserved for the director. The director added his vision and art to the author's, thus coming up with what was shot on film. With sound films, it is still referred to as "direction" but in the screenwriter's format only.

Direction is typed flush at the left-hand margin and runs the full width of the page. It is separated by a double space from the slug line and another double space to a line of direction or character name. It is written in prose, in the present tense, in the active voice and, generally, in simple declarative sentences. Use standard English grammar and correct spelling. Consult *The Chicago Manual of Style* on any matters concerning proper usage.

In direction, the author minimally describes characters. The same goes for objects. (Don't write "1938 Packard convertible" if a simple, "car," will do, unless it's germane to the plot.)

Direction describes singly or in combination the answers to "who," "what," "where" and "when." Only the "why" is missing because you are not telling the camera how to capture the scene. Use enough detail to be accurate about what you see happening in your mind's eye; don't be repetitive.

D

A page black with direction is daunting. Additionally, the same can be said for "talking heads" scenes (pages full of dialogue). Break long descriptions into three-, four- or five-sentence paragraphs. Really effective, fast-moving action can be achieved by a series of one-sentence descriptions.

Always temper your direction with intelligence.

Barring that, temper it with common sense.

If not that, make it short.

Be generous in your economy of words.

Start another paragraph when the subject changes.

Start another paragraph when the action changes.

Abbreviate titles, such as Mr., Dr., Capt., Sgt.

In direction, be creative and innovative. As a screenwriter you tell a story by instigating visual images. From that, it all begins.

D

DIRECTION AND ACTION

The description of the action that takes place.

Boredom must be avoided at all costs. Want to write the world's longest sentence? Do it in a novel, not here. Use quick-talk. Short sentences. One-word slug lines. Grab the reader by the nose, and pull him along with you. Something like this:

BATTER

  . . . swinging at the pitch with all his might as —

RUNNER AT FIRST

starts to go when —

BATTER

sees it's a lousy hit, but a terrific bunt and —

CATCHER

as he's caught by surprise and falls back on his butt with —

THIRD BASE COACH

shouting, signaling the third base runner as —

BATTER

takes off for first base and —

DUGOUT

the manager waving his arms, screaming and —

STADIUM

standing, cheering and —

D

One way to write good description and action is to take a cue from chess—don't make a move that isn't necessary, vital or without purpose. In your descriptions, the sentences should contain critical information. For instance:

```
The rookie walks off the field, slams his bat into
the rack, tears off his helmet and throws it
against the wall, then kicks the water fountain.
```

Readers don't need internalization or subtext to know what's going on with that character, and the writer does not take a chance with a director who feels the rookie's anger can best be expressed with a protracted pout.

If paragraphs start running into four, five or six lines, break them up into shorter ones.

Think of writing description and action as putting your narrative on a super-express highway: camera directions, excess verbiage, unnecessary description, etc., act like tollbooths, bringing everything to a stop. That should happen only in the right place in your script—at THE END. This is easier if you remind yourself to trust the several other creative people who have a crack at your screenplay, including but not limited to, the director, talent, cameraman, scenic and graphic designers, costumer.

D

DIRECTION AND CHARACTERS

When a character is introduced for the first time, the CHAR-ACTER NAME is typed in capital letters. It is also typed in capitals in slug lines, captions, and each time the character has dialogue. The name is in upper and lower case when typed in descriptions and within dialogue. Use the same name throughout the script.

The directions should describe the character in a silhouette of substance rather than a detailed police-type drawing. Generally, that means sex, age bracket, body structure, posture or anything unique, such as eye patch, goatee, tattoo. The more important the character, the more detail. But, don't go overboard. (Where would anyone find a 6'4" blonde, green-eyed, prepossessing teenager? Would you like to have your script wait on a shelf until such an actress was discovered?)

The author also describes the settings here. As much or as little description is given to accurately convey the author's vision.

DIRECTION AND OBJECTS

D

This should not be looked at as an opportunity to create an inventory. If you mention an object, e.g., weapons, paintings, canes, teapots, it must be vital to the film—for ambience or plot. If you focus on a prop, the general rule is that the action (by direction or in dialogue) will return to the object at least once after it has been pointed out because it will become part of the dramatic use of a pointer, arrow or setup inserted earlier, to be used later. (This is part of the theater rule that says if you are going to use a weapon in Act III, you must show it to the audience in Act I so the audience won't be surprised when they see it, and you must use it in Act III.)

The object may be indicated in the same format as a slug line, followed by a description of it, especially what you want the camera to "see."

D DIRECTION AND SETTINGS

There is more to the depiction of a setting than its physical properties. I'm sure you've been in a restaurant with "atmosphere." What gives it that ambience? That's what you should try to bring out when depicting a setting. It should not be overblown, poetic, or even merely adequate. The art director will add his knowhow if you merely let your needs be known.

ELLIPSIS MARKS

Three spaced dots indicate words omitted in dialogue.

The three dots are always typed with three dots and four spaces: space-dot-space-dot-space-dot-space. That is standard English usage.

Technically, the ellipsis marks—or points— are used when there is an omission from a quotation. It has been subrogated by writers to indicate an incomplete thought.

```
                    NANCY
          I was just wondering . . .
```

If dialogue is interrupted by personal direction, the ellipsis marks must continue on the next line of dialogue:

```
                    NANCY
          I wanted to see . . .
                 (winces)
          . . . and I'm glad I did.
```

The correct use of ellipsis marks is when a sentence is started and the end of it is omitted. The omission is shown with the ellipsis marks, and the period is shown as the last (fourth) dot:

```
                    NANCY
          I had to know . . . .
```

Other punctuation, i.e., exclamation point, question mark, typed before or after the ellipses marks follows the same usage as the period in the above example.

Some studios, publishers and typists do not use the spaces between the ellipsis marks; this is simply to save space, not because it is correct English usage.

(Note: An ellipsis—where an understood word is omitted in a sentence (such as: "If (it is) open (you) walk in.")—and ellipsis *marks* are not the same thing.)

E

END

The ending of the script requires two elements: "FADE OUT." and "THE END."

"FADE OUT" appears in all capital letters. It is typed two spaces down, after the last line of direction or dialogue, in the transitional column, left-aligned at 7-1/2". It is followed by six spaces, and the words "THE END," which are centered in the dialogue column, typed in all capital letters.

If you're tight for space, use fewer than six spaces to close out the script.

An example:

```
                    LUDVINNIA
          Yes, you're right. It would be
          difficult to prove I am the widow
          of the Unknown Soldier.

                                   FADE OUT.




               THE END
```

ENTER/EXIT

E

Entrances and exits are written in direction and typed in upper and lower case letters. They are not typed in all capital letters, as in playwriting. For example:

```
The cowpoke enters the bar through the swinging
doors, has a drink at the bar, and exits through
the side door.
```

E

ESTABLISHING SHOT

Identifies immediately the locale or where we are in the story.

The Establishing Shot is found in the slug line. The location may serve as the slug line's sole purpose and therefore it may stand as a solitary slug line, without direction or dialogue. It may also indicate there is a STOCK SHOT available. An example:

```
EXT. THE EMPIRE STATE BUILDING - DAY - ESTABLISH-
ING - STOCK (?)

EXT. THE BOWERY - DAY
```

EXTERIOR

A vital, basic, master slug line component. Along with its opposite (INTERIOR), it comprises one of the three major components of the slug line . The other two components are "DAY/NIGHT" and locale.

Use of "EXTERIOR" immediately tells where the scene takes place—outdoors rather than indoors. It is always abbreviated "EXT." in the slug line and it shares the first place in a slug line with "INTERIOR" (abbreviated "INT".), if applicable. "EXT." is required in a primary slug line introducing a scene, but is omitted if it is redundant in a secondary slug line introducing a shot in the ongoing scene. An example:

```
EXT. BRENDA'S PATIO - DAY
```

This may be the primary slug line introducing a scene, so when the shot changes to the swimming pool, the slug line would then read:

```
SWIMMING POOL
```

continued on next page

E

EXTERIOR *continued from previous page*

At times, " EXT." is used together with "INT." (written "EXT./ INT".), when two or more adjacent areas are used in a scene. For example, a character that is indoors may walk outdoors. Or, two characters may be speaking to each other, one indoors and the other outdoors. If the action of the scene moves from inside the front door onto the porch, the slug line would read:

```
EXT./INT. LUDVINNIA'S PORCH - DAY
```

or:

```
INT./EXT. CAVE ENTRANCE - NIGHT

Throckmorton walks out of the cave, lights the
torch from the fire outside the entrance, turns,
pushes the gondola several feet into the cave.
```

or:

```
EXT./INT. LUDVINNIA'S PORCH - DAY

Ludvinnia walks up the steps, checks the mailbox,
opens the front door and enters. Throckmorton
grabs her from behind, turns her, and kisses her
passionately.
```

EXTREME LONG SHOT

A camera angle.

Again, do not use this or any camera angle unless absolutely necessary. This is the director's province.

F FADE IN/FADE OUT

"FADE IN:" opens a screenplay. It is found only on the first page, typed flush-left and three spaces down from the centered title. It uses a colon. "FADE IN:" is followed by a double space. The trend is not to begin with "FADE IN:."

"FADE OUT" ends a screenplay. It is typed left-aligned at 6-1/2", three spaces down from the script's last line and uses a period. Three to six spaces down, it is followed by the centered, capitalized words: "THE END."

"FADE IN:" should not be confused with the camera direction "FADE TO:" which is sometimes used to close acts.

FIVE-AND-DIME TREATMENT

F

A New York underground simplified method of judging a screenplay by looking at the first five pages and the last ten pages.

If you've spent weeks or months writing a script, you may well resent the arrogance of this practice. Yet, considering that anyone with a word processor or pencil and paper can be a "screenwriter;" that with the vast number of screenplays being written, filmmakers or contest judges can select from any number of well-written scripts; and that the technique is based on the philosophy that you don't have to eat the whole egg to know it's rotten, you may understand the rationalization for such treatment.

So, writers: take the challenge. Dare to make your story—and, especially its opening—a smash. Be sure to close with a climactic scene and create an ending that leaves the reader both satisfied and content.

The best revenge for the five-and-dime treatment is to write a great story. So, don't send out anything but your very, very best effort and make sure that, at the very least, your first five and last ten pages are explosive!

FLY PAGE or TITLE PAGE

This appears immediately after the script cover. It is an informational page containing limited but specific information. The title of the screenplay appears one-third down from the top, centered and in all capital letters. Centered three spaces below the title, typed in upper and lower case letters is, "Screenplay by". (Some authors opt to write "by" instead of "Screenplay by".) Centered three spaces below that, typed in upper and lower case letters is the author's name. Also noted on the title page is other screenplay information, i.e., if the story is an adaptation or translation.

In the lower right-hand corner, on separate, single-spaced lines, type the name, address, phone and fax numbers of the author of the script or the owner of the script or the author's representative. This is known as the "Source Address."

Following is an example of a fly (or title) page:

```
                      (top of page)




                    DEATH BY DESIRE

                    Screenplay by

              Throckmorton T. Throckmorton




                              T. T. Throckmorton
                              5 Independence Street
                              Columbia IA 50057
                              Tel: (515) 555-1212
                              Fax: (515) 555-1234

                    (bottom of page)
```

FOREGROUND (f.g.)

A slug line stage direction, it focuses on and directs the viewer to the closest action in a large scene. If it is used at the start of a sentence, capitalize the "f."

With its companion, "BACKGROUND (b.g.)," here are examples:

```
In the b.g. the enemy tank CLANKS around the far
corner with its cannon firing, machine gun going.
F.g. shows the soldier struggling to reach the
rocket launcher.
```

or:

```
In the f.g., the tank's gun turret swings around
toward the soldier. In the b.g. we see and hear
the SOUND of a dive bomber going high-pitch.
```

F

FOREIGN LANGUAGE

When a foreign language is spoken or foreign accent is to be used, it is indicated in the talent or dialogue column by a parenthetical in the dialogue element. It is followed by the dialogue in English. Underline foreign words and phrases wherever they appear. An example:

                    THROCKMORTON
                (in a French accent)
        When it comes to <u>haute couture</u> and
        mayonnaise I am an expert. It's
        dressing, you see?

Following is an example of when a foreign language is used and subtitles are called for:

                    THROCKMORTON
                (in French with
                English subtitles)
        This gourmet would like a hot dog.

INSERT

Used when the writer wishes to focus attention on a very specific object for a specific reason. It is a shot within a shot.

For example, the author may wish to indicate the time by going to an insert of a clock on a wall. To end an insert, follow the guidelines for "POV": use "BACK TO SCENE", go to a dialogue element or switch to a new location. Here's an example:

```
INSERT - BOMB

Between the books, the clock on the sticks of dy-
namite shows there are twenty seconds to go.

BACK TO SCENE
```

or:

```
INSERT - LETTER

The tweezers point to the dot in the letterhead.

POLICE STATION
```

INTERCUT

A direction indicating two or more separate but simultaneous locations. Use it sparingly. (See also MATCH CUT, page 87.)

As a slug line direction it may be written:

THROCKMORTON'S BEDROOM/NANCY'S BEDROOM

We INTERCUT between their phone conversation.

or:

INTERCUTTING

Throckmorton and Nancy in their bedrooms, the killer in a phone booth.

or:

THROCKMORTON AND NANCY

The scene INTERCUTS between Throckmorton at an airport telephone and Nancy in her bedroom.

INTERIOR

A vital, basic master slug line component, it shares one of the three major slug line components with "EXTERIOR." (The other two components are "DAY/NIGHT" and locale.)

Interior means indoors rather than outdoors. In the slug line, it is always abbreviated "INT." It immediately indicates that the scene takes place inside a structure of some sort—a home, a barn, a boat, a plane, a cave, a space vehicle—anyplace indoors. Like its "EXT." counterpart, "INT." is required in a master slug line that introduces a scene, but it is omitted in secondary slug lines of an ongoing scene. An example:

```
INT. HOTEL BAR - NIGHT
```

This is the master slug line. But, when the shot changes to a booth, the slug line would then read:

```
BOOTH
```

See EXTERIOR, page 69.

L LIVESTOCK

Refers to animals and anything that goes along with them, such as stage coaches, wagons, stone boats. Be specific only if it is germane to do so. An example:

```
Livestock, standing, lying on the ground, are
scattered across the quiet battlefield.
```

LONG SHOT

L

A camera angle indicating a distant view. It is not generally used in the author's script. Instead, find another way to give this camera direction, such as:

```
In the far distance, we can see the avalanche
start down the mountain.
```

M

MACRO

A computer term meaning a "customized," two- or three-key-stroke operation used to perform a repetitive task (which may otherwise require a multitude of keystrokes).

In effect, macros are computer shorthand and are used to create a screenplay writing program. Macros can be generated on a word processing application program and can be used for any number of tasks. (I use "macro" as an acronym for "Make A Computer Repetition Order.")

The macro is a cousin of the tab key and it works in a similar manner. The "tab" key was derived from the typewriter's "tabu-lator" bar, which was used to hop horizontally across a page, from one column of figures or listings to the next. The tab key's purpose has not changed: in word processing, whenever the tab key is pressed, it jumps the cursor a preset number of spaces. So, instead of pounding out the spaces one at a time, the cursor moves five, ten, or any other preset number of spaces, from tab stop to tab stop. A macro can store a sequence of keystrokes, thereby recording and rerunning commands—simple or complex—when called upon to do so.

One of the great features of a macro is that whether you use it once or a thousand times, it will faithfully perform without an error. In addition, once you have expended the energy in cre-ating a macro, you never have to do that work again.

I created a screenwriting program with macros. For instance, I made macros for the following tasks:

• Skipping two spaces;

• Typing a Character Name (one for each character in my screenplay);

• Setting the dialogue margins, allowing me to use word wrap and to insert parentheticals;

• Returning to the direction column with the proper margins at the end of the dialogue.

Most macros are created in the same way:

- Enter the keystrokes requesting the creation of a macro.

- Give the macro an identifying name or code which is used to recall that macro whenever it is needed.

- Enter the precise operation, however short or complicated, such as, making a Character Name for each character, along with the accompanying format margins.

- Close the macro.

Most of today's word processing programs are able to create macros. It behooves you to become macro literate. Take your word processor to a higher level—create macros.

M MANUSCRIPT LENGTH

One page of a screenplay is roughly equal to one minute of screen time. A full-length screenplay runs around 120 pages, although acceptable length can be anywhere from 90 to 130 pages.

MARGINS

M

The top margin should be 1". The bottom margin may vary from 1/2" to 1-1/2", depending on the most convenient place to stop. The left-hand margin should be 1-1/2", to be sure the script is not obscured by the cover and fasteners. The right-hand margin should be 1". Page numbers are typed 1/2" down from the top margin. From the left margin to the right, there should be about 6 inches. These page margins should not vary much—they may alter the timing yardstick (one page per one minute of screen time).

Margins for the screenplay page are:

SLUG LINE begins 1-1/2" from the left edge of the page;

DIRECTION and DESCRIPTION also begin at the same place as the Slug Line;

DIALOGUE begins at 2-1/2" and ends at 5-1/2".

PARENTHETICALS begin at 3" and extend no further than 5-1/2".

CHARACTER NAMES begin at 3-1/2".

TRANSITIONAL INSTRUCTIONS begin at 6-1/2" and are left-aligned.

M MASTER SCENE

Screenplays are written from the point of view of one master scene to another. The locale of that master scene is a critical element of the slug line and calls for the shortest, clearest identification possible. A master scene slug line must contain "INT." and/or "EXT."; and "DAY" or "NIGHT".

A master scene may consist of one shot or it can be a series of shots. For example, a master scene may be of a single shot of an apple pie. Or, a master scene may consist of shots of the various slices that make up the pie. Or, those slices may be termed subsidiary scenes and headed by subsidiary slug lines.

There are a variety of slug lines or scene headings which may be used in a master scene.

See SLUG LINES, page 123.

MATCH CUT

M

Used to segue between or bridge two scenes by focusing on an inanimate object. It is used to indicate a change in time, location or character by "matching" the same object.

Use "MATCH CUT:" sparingly. As with "CUT TO:" a page may be ended with "MATCH CUT:" but it should not be used to begin a page.

"MATCH CUT:" is typed in all capital letters and followed by a colon. It is placed in the right-hand (transitional) column. An example:

TRUMPET

is in Throckmorton's hands; he's passing it to the pawnbroker.

                                          MATCH CUT:

TRUMPET

is shown again.

INT. CAFE - NIGHT

Nancy holds out the trumpet to Throckmorton.

continued on next page

M

MATCH CUT *continued from previous page*

As a direction, "MATCH CUT:" can be used to indicate the passing of time. For example:

```
INT. BAR - DAY

Throckmorton and Nancy are at a table. Nancy takes
out a cigarette. Throckmorton reaches over.

LIGHTER

It lights, and moves to Nancy's cigarette, and is
put on a clean table.

                                        MATCH CUT:

LIGHTER

rests among empty bottles and glasses.

BAR - NIGHT

Nancy crushes an empty pack of cigarettes.
```

MONTAGE

A series of short, disparate images, showing an association of ideas. In a film, a montage rarely has dialogue. It usually offers individual shots which represent an overview of larger action. When a montage is included, the shots are indicated individually; there should be a space between all elements. For example:

```
MONTAGE

A) Photograph of a football team

B) Car racing a train to a crossing

C) Masked nurse wheeling a gurney

D) Gruesome faces of young adults in pain

END OF MONTAGE
```

Montage is often confused with and used interchangeably with "SERIES OF SHOTS". The prime distinction is that in a "SERIES OF SHOTS" the main character(s) are in a majority of the shots.

The trend today is to simplify, so the lettering (A, B, C) or numbering of views may be dropped.

M   MORE

In a screenplay, "(MORE)" is used when a character's speech is interrupted by the end of the page and is continued onto the next page. "(MORE)" is used only in the talent (dialogue) column.

"(MORE)" was a newspaperman's term used at the bottom of a page of copy to indicate there was more to the story. In screenwriting, it tells us there is more dialogue.

MOS

Action is performed without sound, specifically speech.

A script may say:

```
In the b.g. the students talk MOS.
```

You can use "MOS" in a series of shots. An example:

```
SERIES OF SHOTS - MOS

A. Throckmorton holding a flare gun checks his
   wristwatch

B. Commando sliding under barbed wire

C. Ludvinnia treading water by the bridge, twists
   wires

BACK TO SCENE
```

"MOS" supposedly was derived from early film days. It should have been "WOS," for Without Sound, but the "with" was mispronounced by a German director as "mit." I use it as an acronym for "Make Only Silence."

M   MUSIC

Music engenders emotional involvement. But, unless your choice is made for a very specific reason, be vague. Calling for specific music is restrictive and may throttle a reader's good feeling about your script. Music is trendy and may not be in vogue by the time your movie is made. Or, it may be too expensive to obtain the rights or to have an orchestra record the piece you've named. The writer who simply states: MU-SIC—something light, airy and bubbly! deserves a Bravo! and Encore!

NIGHT/DAY

A vital component of the master slug line, it shares one of the three major components with "DAY" (the other two components are "EXT./INT." and locale).

"DAY" or "NIGHT" is required in a master slug line introducing a scene but is omitted in a secondary slug line in an ongoing scene. Night refers to the light source. In this case, it covers all artificial light and the hours of darkness. In the slug line it is always separated from the locale with a hanging hyphen, and spelled out. It immediately tells that the scene takes place in what is supposed to be light that is available at night, either natural light as from the moon or stars, artificial light as from incandescent or fluorescent bulbs, a night fire, or what have you. It also puts the scene at nighttime. It always shares a place as applicable after the locale with NIGHT.

An example:

EXT. SAILBOAT - NIGHT

N NOTE TO THE DIRECTOR

On those occasions when the author wishes to be absolutely clear about his intent or about a technical detail, he may want to write a note to the director. This is done in the directions, flush with the left-hand column, in parentheses. It begins with "NOTE:" typed in all capitals followed by a colon. The actual note is typed in upper and lower case letters and is separated by a line space above and below. An example:

```
INT. DYNAMITE SHACK - NIGHT

The two men count the sticks of dynamite.

(NOTE: The cigarettes in their mouths are lit.)
```

NUMBERING

The first page of the script is not numbered. Starting on page 2, number pages consecutively. The page number appears in the upper right-hand corner, about 1/2" down, about 1" from the right-hand edge. The Arabic numeral is followed by a period to separate it from the eventual scene numbers that will be put in by the unit production manager.

If changes are made to the script, the inserted page carries the same page number followed by an alphabetical letter. For example, if the inserted pages come after, say, page 18, they are numbered "18A," "18B," and so on.

O OFF SCREEN (O.S.)

Indicating that dialogue or sound is heard but the character speaking or the action creating the sound is not seen on screen. It should not be confused with VOICE OVER (V.O.) which is dialogue from a character not in the scene or in the shot.

"OFF SCREEN" is always abbreviated, typed in all capital letters, with periods. It follows on the same line as the character name and is placed in parentheses. If it appears in the directions, it is typed "O.S." (without parentheses). In the first example below, "O.S." appears beside the character name; in the second, it appears in the directions.

```
                    CHARLES (O.S.)
          I'd like to know if I may open the
          door and come on in?

We HEAR the car crash O.S.
```

"OFF CAMERA" or "O.C." may be used interchangeably with off stage.

See VOICE OVER, page 140.

PAGE ONE

The page number does not appear on Page 1. The first page of the screenplay should contain the following:

- The title of the screenplay is centered and typed in all capital letters, six spaces from the top margin.

- Double-space. Flush with the left-hand margin, in all capital letters, type the direction "FADE IN:" if you choose to use it. This is the first and only time this slug line is used in the screenplay.

- Double-space to the opening slug line.

- If the opening slug line uses "ESTABLISHING," double-space to the next slug line.

- The copyright notice may be written at the bottom of the page, flush with the left-hand margin.

continued on next page

P

PAGE ONE *continued from previous page*

An example:

                    (first page of a screenplay)

                                              (no pg #)

(Six spaces down:)
            THE TITLE, IN CAPS, IS CENTERED

(Double-space:)
FADE IN:

(Double-space:)
MASTER SHOT SLUG LINE GOES HERE   (TIME, if used)

(Double space:)
NEXT SLUG LINE OR DIRECTION OR CHARACTER NAME

        Copyright notice goes here
         - All Rights Reserved -

                    (end of page)

PAN

Short for panorama, this is a comprehensive, unobstructed view of a region. When a camera "pans," it takes in a wide scene without stopping to focus on any one view.

It is a camera direction and therefore is not generally used in an author's script. The author should find another way to indicate it, such as:

```
The sailor's eyes swept the horizon, taking in the
vast armada that lay before him.
```

P

PARENTHETICALS

Brief comment or direction concerning the speaker, relating specifically to that character's action or personal direction.

Parentheticals are indented from the left-hand dialogue column and typed, in lowercase letters, in the center dialogue or talent element. They should "wraparound" from the right-hand column. Such as:

```
              THROCKMORTON
          (this is a parenthetical
          which wraps around)
     His speech would run the full
     three-and-a-half-inch centered
     column.
              (additional parentheticals
              in the same speech follow
              the same rules)
```

Anything longer than two lines should be written as direction before or after the character's dialogue.

A page must not end on a parenthetical; it must stay with the dialogue.

Personal direction parentheticals include "beat" (which indicates a short lapse of time); "sotto voce" (which is a comment the character utters to himself but is said audibly for dramatic effect); and when dialogue is in a foreign accent or foreign language. Another kind of parenthetical direction is when the author wants the character to speak a line a particular way, such as, "angrily," "mockingly" or "indignantly." See DIALOGUE, page 55.

Directors dislike personal direction and actors are loathe to discard their first reading impression. The argument is, good writing dictates the mood of the action. If you feel you should give the actor personal direction, then insert it as part of the directions (and perhaps the director won't notice), such as:

```
                    THROCKMORTON
          I can't do that, no matter what you
          say!
```

He smirks, glances at the gun. Cheek twitching, he stares into the man's eyes. His hand trembles, then it moves for the weapon.

When two or more parentheticals are needed for the same character in the same speech, do not use multiple parentheses; rather, put the directions on the same line with a hyphen in- between. An example:

```
                    LUDVINNIA
              (smiling - waving)
```

or:

```
                    LUDVINNIA
              (nodding - then smiling)
```

Exceptions are: when using "(continuing)" combined with a personal direction, or when using "(beat)" with a personal direction. Then, the two parentheticals are separated not by a hyphen but by a semicolon. Examples:

```
                    LUDVINNIA
              (continuing; a beat)
```

or:

```
                    LUDVINNIA
              (a beat; then waving)
```

P

PERSONAL DIRECTION

An indication of the manner in which a character should appear, behave or react; an indication of the character's tone of speech. It is one of two types of parentheticals; the other is the "action parenthetical."

Personal direction borders on directing, but there are times when it must be used for clarity. For example, to indicate sarcasm, contempt or anger.

See PARENTHETICALS, page 100.

POINT OF VIEW (POV)

The position from which one character involved in the action takes in a scene; what the character sees; what the viewer sees through the character's eyes. With a "POV" the dialogue is heard "(O.S.)" (meaning, off screen—the actor speaking is not seen on screen). See also VOICE OVER, page 140.

The slug line in a "POV" must achieve three essential facts:

1. Identify the shot as a POV;

2. Identify whose POV it is, that is, whose eyes are we looking through; and

3. Identify what the POV sees.

When the POV switches within the same scene, it is referred to as "REVERSE POV."

In the example that follows, first we see only Franco and hear the Presidente. Then, with the REVERSE POV, we hear only Franco and see the Presidente:

```
PRESIDENTE'S POV - FRANCO
He looks across the desk at Franco.

                    PRESIDENTE (O.S.)
          . . . so what did he say was the
          difference between a pit bull and
          my mistress?

REVERSE POV

                    FRANCO (O.S.)
          Lipstick.

The Presidente slowly nods his head several times.

                                        CUT TO:

INT. TORTURE CHAMBER - NIGHT
```

continued on next page

POINT OF VIEW *continued from previous page*

"POV" is a valuable element. It is one of the elements that distinguishes between writing for the stage and writing for the screen. (The stage play calls for action, the screenplay for reaction—we see the effect of the words or action on the listener's face.) POV focuses exactly on that.

In the script any "POV" must be terminated. For example, a slug line—any slug line—will end a "POV." In the example above, if we wanted to end the Presidente's POV, we could use his name in a slug line without additional directions:

```
PRESIDENTE'S POV - FRANCO

He looks across the desk at Franco.

PRESIDENTE
```

The second "PRESIDENTE" stops the "POV" and the shot with directions or dialogue continues.

Another example:

```
COP'S POV - THE CROWD

comes charging down the street.

                                    CUT TO:
```

"BACK TO SCENE" also may be used to end a "POV."

Note that neither an inanimate object nor more than one character can be the source of a "POV." Authors and directors are known to hedge on this point via poetic license. For example, a shot will focus on the eye of a bird, and then we'll see a shot of a city from high above, as if it's from the bird's POV. Without that, through whose eyes are we seeing the scene?

Another note: "POV" is a camera angle.

PRIMARY SLUG

P

Used to introduce or begin master scenes. You may run across the terms "PRIMARY SLUG" and "SECONDARY SLUG" in some screenwriting guides or computer programs. Primary slugs lines introduce the master scene; secondary (or, subsidiary) slug lines are used for the shots within a master scene.

P   PRODUCTION SCRIPT

The script being shot. A production script has many technical requirements. Although absolutely necessary for production of the film, these technical requirements would be a burden in an author's script and so they are not usually included.

As a screenwriter, you may be curious about what a production script looks like. I recommend Pauline Kael's *Raising Kane*, which includes the history of the script to CITIZEN KANE, the shooting script and the cutting continuity of the completed film. May every screenwriter see his work turned into a production script.

PROPS

P

The abbreviation for properties, the term is derived from the theater and is defined as any inanimate article or object used in a scene. Props are the set pieces needed for the "business" of the shot.

Props may be anything held or used in the scene, e.g., furniture, paintings, dishes or personal items such as attache cases, purses, handkerchiefs, canes. Painted scenery and costumes are not props. A general rule is that anything handled by an actor in a scene is considered a prop. All else is scenery or set decoration.

"SLAPS" is a bookkeeping theater entry acronym covering the expenses for "Sets, Lights, and Properties."

Q QUERY LETTER

A brief, broad pitch of your screenplay and a request for a release form. Enclose a self-addressed, stamped envelope with your query. If it receives a positive response and you send your script, indicate the following on the script's envelope: "Requested Ms." and "Release Enclosed."

A query letter is one page. Summarize your script in one short paragraph. State your writing credits briefly but skip this part if you don't have any. Ask for a release form which, in effect, says if someone at the production company steals your idea, you won't blame them.

REGISTRATION

R

A service offered by the Writers Guild of America for a fee. It is not an official COPYRIGHT, but can be used to establish date of ownership. For information on registering your screenplay, write to:

Writers Guild of America, West
7000 West Third Street
Los Angeles, CA 90048
Telephone 213-782-4520

or:

Writers Guild of America, East
555 West 57th Street
New York, NY 10019
Telephone 212-767-7800

The web site for the Writers Guild of America is http://www.wga.org. For writers outside of the United States of America, the WGA maintains links to international writers guilds (e.g., Writers Guild of Canada, Writers Guild of Great Britain).

S | SASE

The acronym or abbreviation for "self-addressed, stamped envelope." Along with the script and SASE, always include a cover letter.

Never send your script to anyone without an SASE, especially if you want your script returned. There are some organizations, producers and contests that will not return a script, even with an SASE attached; this is especially true if you have sent your script out blindly—that is, if you did not pave the way with a query letter. Also, not returning scripts minimizes the company's legal responsibilities.

Make sure you enclose enough postage to cover the return of your script and make sure the return envelope is large enough to hold it. And, if you send your script out of the country, you must purchase and enclose International Coupons for the correct amount of return postage.

SCENE ENDINGS

There are several ways you can end a scene.

"CUT TO:" is a scene ender but since it is assumed that most scenes would end with it, it is not popularly used. However, it is used when there is a dramatic shift in locale, time or action.

"MATCH CUT:" is a direction that segues or bridges two scenes by focusing on an inanimate object, indicating a change in time, location or character.

Do not use other scene endings, such as "DISSOLVE:" "DISSOLVE TO:" "MATCH DISSOLVE TO:" "SLAM CUT:" "JUMP CUT:" These belong in the province of the director; use them at your risk.

SCENE HEADING or SLUG LINE

Part of the direction element, it is used to introduce a new scene.

It should stand out, so it is always typed in capital letters. There is a double-space before a slug line and a double-space after it. It begins flush with the left-hand column. It is never "orphaned" (left alone) at the bottom of a page.

A slug line is usually one line, but there are occasions when it will go to a second line. If this happens, it should be typed directly under the first line, without any spaces skipped. Make the break at a logical place (such as a hyphen) at the end of the first line.

A master scene slug line gives the reader three important pieces of information: .

• Whether the scene takes place inside or outside ("INT." or "EXT.");

• The scene's locale;

• Whether it's night or day.

Slug lines also are used to indicate shots within master scenes; these are called "subsidiary" or "secondary" slug lines and they indicate the beginning of a shot. Some examples:

```
EXT. CAR MOVING THROUGH ESTATE COUNTRY - LONG IS-
LAND - DAY

INT. THE MOVING CAR - DAY

INT. ENTRANCE AND FAMILY ROOM - LUDVINNIA'S HOUSE
- NIGHT
```

In between master slug lines, there may be one shot or many.

If a scene moves from indoors to outdoors, the slug line would read: "INT./EXT." For example:

```
EXT./INT. DEPARTMENT STORE ENTRANCE - DAY
```

A subsidiary slug line does not carry redundant information, so, generally it would consist of the location only, as they are continuations of the master scene. In the final shooting script, the unit production manager (UPM) will add in the necessary Interior/Exterior and Day/Night information.

Qualifying elements, known as "extensions," may be added to slug lines, if necessary. These would include:

• time or season for either the locale or the film;

• if a "stock" shot is used;

• if the shot is "ESTABLISHING" in either location or time of day. "Establishing" is used almost always at the beginning of the film to immediately establish the general locale of the story. It is also a subtle way to kick-start the viewer's "suspension of disbelief." The "Establishing" shot slug line may stand by itself and it is the only slug line that may be followed by another slug line. It need not be followed by directions, descriptions or dialogue. For example:

```
EXT. NEW YORK CITY - DAY - ESTABLISHING    (FALL)
```

Extensions deal with time—past, present, future. "Present" always means today's world or, the day the movie is being made. "Future" can be a specific year or can be a general time. If you intend a specific year, then you must indicate the specific year.

```
EXT. CEMETERY - NIGHT (TIME: FUTURE)
```

or:

```
INT. AIRPORT - EARLY MORNING (PRESENT)
```

or:

```
EXT. RIVER - NIGHT (WINTER 1776)
```

continued on next page

S

SCENE HEADING or SLUG LINE *continued from previous page*

Whoever reads the script will know it is "WINTER 1776," but how will the movie audience come to know this? One way is to superimpose the time period onto the screen. Or, you can find a way to indicate it in your directions.

Here's another example involving time:

```
INT. THE MANSE (1944) - NIGHT
```

This slug line tells you the scene takes place inside a home, at night, with a date specific to the location (and not to the remainder of the screenplay). The date qualifies the location.

Shooting scripts may indicate camera angles in scene headings.

A slug line may contain the character's name or the characters who are involved in the scene (provided we have already been introduced to them in a prior scene). Also, a slug line may be used as the beginning of a sentence. An example:

```
THROCKMORTON AND LUDVINNIA

stare into each other's eyes as they walk off the
end of the pier, MOS.
```

Here are two different ways you can say the same thing. In the first example, the action is indicated in the directions:

```
Throckmorton is at the wheel of a boat, racing
along.
```

Or, you can indicate it in a scene heading:

```
THROCKMORTON DRIVING BOAT - SPEEDING
```

Use whatever it takes to do the very best for your script.

SCREEN CREDIT

That which is given to people involved in the making of a film. Credits (or titles) may be shown on the screen at any time—before the film begins, at the beginning of the film or at the end of it.

If they are shown during the film, they must be superimposed or printed in a particular spot selected by the director, usually in conjunction with the film editor. The screenplay's author does not usually indicate where the credits should be shown. It is acceptable to mark "MAIN TITLES BEGIN" and "MAIN TITLES END" if the author feels it is essential to the opening.

S

SCREENPLAY DEFINED

The manuscript form of a story prepared in a traditional, "screen-play" format which presents the unique elements required for the production of a motion picture, including but not limited to a description of characters, details of scenes and settings, dialogue, stage direction or action.

A screenplay has also been defined as a story told in pictures.

SCREENPLAY PAGE

When the first script was written, three elements (in addition to the actual screenplay) were necessary: a director; the talent; a camera. For quick and easy identification of these elements, each was assigned a place vertically on the script page.

The director got the lion's share of the page—the information that went completely across the page. Today, any information that begins at the left-hand margin and runs across the page is known as "direction." Under direction are slug lines, descriptive passages for action, characters, atmosphere, views and events.

When talkies arrived, cue cards would no longer be usable so space was found on the page for the dialogue. Talent received the center third of the page. Here we find character names, dialogue and parenthetical comments. The right-hand third of the page was reserved for the transitional elements, or camera directions, i.e., the camera makes a transition from one shot to the next. Some camera directions include "CUT TO:" and "FADE OUT."

SCRIPT SPECIFICATIONS

Don't challenge the reader by presenting an unprofessional, sloppily prepared, poorly formatted script. The following rules apply:

• Always use white paper. Cream is not white. You may see scripts with different colored paper for various drafts. This is done only after the script is optioned and goes into rewrite; there is a specific order of colored paper for draft copies. Draft or otherwise, never submit a script on anything but white paper.

• Always use 20-lb. paper stock. If your computer paper is thin or of poor quality, photocopy the script onto heavier, better paper.

• Always use the standard paper size of 8-1/2" x 11".

• When photocopying your script, it is now acceptable to copy on both sides of the paper. It is much easier to have your local copy shop do this for you, than to try to do it your self on your own printer. Keep your original, one-sided copy as a master.

• Pages must be numbered consecutively. Inserted pages should carry the page number they follow, with letters A, B, C, and so on.

• Always use a letter-quality printer. Your best bet is a laser printer or laser-quality (inkjet printer). The printing/typing/photocopying must be in jet black ink with no broken letters and no ink-clogged letters (such as the E, D or O). Don't use a fancy font. The standard Courier 12 point (10 pitch) is generally accepted.

• Do not "justify" the right-hand margin. It makes the page look neat, but it also makes the page difficult to read.

• Do not hyphenate words at the end of a line. Along the same line, do not split a sentence from one page to the next.

• All scripts should be properly bound. (See BINDING, page 38.)

• Spell out all numbers (such as three million dollars or $3 million) and the time of day but use numbers in directions. If you must indicate time of day (i.e., a.m. and p.m.), use instead, ". . . in the morning," or, ". . . at night." Spell out all personal titles, except Mr., Mrs., Ms., Sgt., Lt., Capt. Be sure to spell out a title that may be misread, such as "Colonel" or "Monsignor."

• Send your script through spell check but read it carefully for homonyms.

S | SENDING OUT SCRIPTS

Clear the way for your script by sending a query letter first (enclose an SASE). Even if you're in a rush to get your script out, you may find that a query is the shortest long way around. Even so, your query may be returned, marked: "Unopened and Unread" (even if the envelope was opened). That will tell you about the litigiously nervous movie business. You may want to indicate that your correspondence is a query letter by writing "QUERY" in the lower left-hand corner of the envelope.

Do not send a script by registered mail. If you want to know if your script has been received, enclose a self-addressed, stamped postcard and ask the story editor to drop the postcard in the mail. To save on postage, some authors mail their scripts with both envelopes marked: "Manuscript - Special Fourth-Class Mail." Others prefer to make a statement and send it first-class both ways. (Even small things carry the mark of the professional. If you're sending out a script that may cost a studio a few million dollars to produce, would they show much enthusiasm for it if you sent it over in your old, recycled envelopes? Of course, none of this matters if your screenplay is magnificent.)

Do not send a summary of your script; the reader must make up his own mind about your work—in an unbiased manner.

See AGENT, page 33.

SERIES OF SHOTS

A number of short action sequences, usually without dialogue, that condense a storyline using the main characters (the basic difference from a MONTAGE). The format is:

• "SERIES OF SHOTS" is the slug line, flush left;

• Skip a space;

• Begin numbering the shots, using capital letters, i.e., A, B, although the trend is not to;

• After each letter, list the shot or a descriptive paragraph of the action you want;

• Use spaces in between descriptions;

• End the series with the slug line, "END SERIES OF SHOTS"

An example:

```
SERIES OF SHOTS

A) Jack and Jill go up a hill to fetch a pail of
   water

B) Jack falls down and breaks his crown

C) Jill comes tumbling after

END SERIES OF SHOTS

                                            CUT TO:
```

S

SEQUENCE

A sequential series of shots, focusing on one theme, that make up the master scene. SIMULTANEOUS BUSINESS; instances when the screenwriter wishes to show that several important elements are going on at the same time, for example, two people talking over each other.

Simultaneous business is easily indicated in stage directions or in side-by-side dialogue columns. But, if you need to indicate three or four actors speaking at the same time, you need more space than four columns of dialogue provides. The "simultaneous" element ends with the "BACK TO SCENE," direction, description, action or another slug line. One way to show simultaneous conversations would be as follows:

SIMULTANEOUS DIALOGUE:

                    THROCKMORTON
          Each character's lines are written
          in standard dialogue format.

                    LUDVINNIA
          They would speak their lines over
          or on top of the other's . . .

                    HARVEY
          . . . using ellipsis marks to slow
          down a speech

                    ESMERELDA
          . . . or to show a delay in deliv-
          ery of a line.

                              BACK TO SCENE

SLUG LINES

The beginning of a scene which gives the most vital information, i.e., interior or exterior; location; day or night.

The slug line is derived from the newspaper; it has been said that the first screenwriter was a maverick reporter who thought up the idea of using familiar terms as a format for screenplay writing. In newspaper lingo, "slugs" are sticks of lead produced by Linotype machines; they are also type lines used to identify blocks of type that already have been set. A reporter's written story or copy would be given a slug line at the editor's desk, such as "Fire," "Governor," "Parade." The slug line then would be used by the headline writer to identify the headline that went with the story. The Linotype operator, who set the story in type, would "slug" the work for identification. The makeup editor would use the slug line to identify the placement of the story and how much space it would take on his "dummy" page of the paper. All of the elements came together in the composing room where the slug lines and their particular components "made up" the newspaper.

Regarding the screenplay, because the camera was king, its needs were met first in the all-important slug-lined information (which identified whether it was an interior or exterior shot; the location of the scene; and what kind of lighting would be needed). Today, in screenplays, the slug is still important.

See SCENE HEADINGS, page 112.

S SOUND CUE

A warning to the sound technician that the reproduction or generation of sound is needed.

The cues are found in the directions; they are typed in all capitals. (For example, they may involve a horn BLOWING, bells RINGING, or indicate a train CRASH.) Usually, the one word describing the sound is capitalized. Sounds that occur in the course of normal action, e.g., dropping a shoe, pounding a nail, are not emphasized. (In other words, generally not those sounds made by characters.)

A cue is a warning, alerting the sound technician that special services are needed. For example:

```
Our hero goes CRASHING through the plate glass
window.
```

or:

```
The CHUG and WHISTLE of the train blocks out the
conversation.
```

See SOUND EFFECTS, page 125.

SOUND EFFECTS (SFX)

Describe in direction the sound effects that must be reproduced (with the sounds themselves typed in all capital letters). For example:

```
INT. RAILROAD STATION WAITING ROOM - DAY

Throckmorton and Ludvinnia are standing. She is
about to speak when the CHUG and WHISTLE of a
locomotive stops her cold.
```

Sound effects do not refer to music.

See SOUND CUES, page 124.

SPACING

The spacing format for screenplays, with only a few minor exceptions, is very simple:

- Direction, character name and dialogue are single-spaced.

- Everything else is double-spaced, i.e., before and after a slug line, a paragraph, a line of direction or dialogue and after "(MORE)."

Exceptions are:

- The first page of a script, when the title is typed six spaces down from the top of the page. Double-space from the title to "FADE IN:" and double-space to the first slug line after "FADE IN:"

- The last page of the script, when you double-space to "FADE OUT." and then move six spaces (or less, if you're tight for space) to "THE END" which is centered.

SPECIAL EFFECTS (FX or SPFX)

With the advancement of technology—not only the computer chip but in compositions of special materials and mechanical contraptions—special effects have taken on a new dimension. Special effects now encompass a new universe of creativity involving prehistoric animals, spaceships, intergalactic bombardments, invading monsters—in other words, they are pure wizardry on the screen.

Before you write a script calling for a huge special effects budget, it is recommended that you show your wondrous gift for screenwriting.

Use direction to present the scene you have in mind:

```
INT. RAILROAD STATION WAITING ROOM - NIGHT - FX

A locomotive derails, crashes, explodes.
```

S | SPINE

Same as the spine of a book, the spine of a screenplay is that area where the edges of the pages are bound together (or, the edges of the script closest to the fasteners). Some authors put identifying numbers on the spines of their scripts to keep track of the copies.

SPLIT SCREEN

S

A device for slicing the screen into several smaller ones. The screen may be split vertically, horizontally or diagonally. For example, each split may show different people in different locations doing different things simultaneously.

"SPLIT SCREEN" is written as a slug line direction and is typed in all capital letters. The author identifies in direction what is seen. An example:

```
SPLIT SCREEN

In six splits, show the Marines landing under fire
on the beach.
```

This technique has been pretty much phased out.

S   STAGE DIRECTION

The same as the element direction, stage direction provides information about any aspect of what's to be seen on the screen. It may relate to the action, situation, talent, location, setting, blocking, movement.

See DIRECTION, page 58.

STOCK SHOTS

S

Archival footage, or shots that have already been filmed, and that are stored for later use.

Stock shots may be used over and over again. They lower the cost of filmmaking because it's cheaper to use a stock shot of, say, a battleship firing its guns, than to film it. Unless you know what stock shots are available, there is no need to use this element. If you feel a stock shot may be available, write stock shot with a question mark in parentheses, such as: "STOCK SHOT (?)."

S SUBJECTIVE CAMERA

Used when the author wishes the audience to see what's on the screen through the eyes of the talent (whether it's a human, animal or monster) that has not yet been introduced on camera.

SUBSIDIARY CHARACTERS

When a subsidiary character is used, identify him by his occupation or activity; this is typed in all capital letters, such as: SALES CLERK, BUS DRIVER, FIREFIGHTER. If more than one minor character of the same occupation or activity is used, number them, such as: SURFBOARDER 1, SURFBOARDER 2, SURFBOARDER 3.

Capitalize the first instance that a subsidiary character is introduced in the script. Unless you have something specific in mind, temper your description of the character with that character's importance to the shot, i.e., if it's a brief role, make it a brief description.

"BITS" refer to cast members with minor parts. "BITS" are used in crowd scenes or atmosphere shots. The theater axiom is, "There are bit parts but no bit actors."

S

SUPERIMPOSE

To show one shot over another. Superimposed shots are used
most often during the running of screen credits. Or, they can
be titles on the film which interpret the dialogue (also known
as subtitles). Or, indications of locale, time or season are often
superimposed.

TALENT

T

Performers.

Talent, or dialogue, occupies the center third of the screenwriting page. It is used for character names, dialogue, parentheticals, continuations and modifiers. Talent can refer to actors both animate and inanimate (human, animal, fish, fowl), real or invented, composited, bionic, actual or imaginary. In other words, "Talent" can refer to almost anything that relates to the cast of a movie. The word, "Talent" is used because it is all-encompassing.

T

TALKING HEADS

Refers to screenplay pages filled almost exclusively with dialogue between two or more characters. This may be acceptable for a stage play, but a "talking heads" scene is deadly for anything but an exceptionally written film.

"Talking heads" are usually a page design problem, as are daunting black pages full of slug lines and direction. Either one puts the screenplay in a tailspin. The author should step back and view the scene(s) with a mind to keeping the pace going at a fast clip while keeping the page in balance.

TITLES

T

The element that lists all crucial information for the film, e.g., title, author, performers, director, producer and any and all other crew members. Titles also may include advisors, acknowledgments, dedications, etc.

Titles may appear at any time during the film: before it starts, at the beginning, middle, end, or after the movie is over. Where the titles appear is the director's province; he usually makes this decision in concert with the film editor.

When mentioning the title of a book, song, movie, TV show or magazine in the script, it should be found in the directions, placed in quotation marks and typed in all capital letters.

See FLY PAGE or TITLE PAGE, page 74.

T | TRANSITIONALS

For camera directions, the transitional element is found on the right-hand third of the page. The information in this column indicates to the cameraman that there is a transition from one shot to another.

At one time, it was very specific as to how the transition was made by a variety of camera angles, shots, directions, including "CRANE SHOT," "CLOSE-UP," "TRUCKING SHOT," "TWO-SHOT," "DOLLY IN," "DOLLY BACK." These are no longer used.

Today, transitionals are limited to a mere handful, including "CUT TO:" "DISSOLVE TO:" "FADE OUT."

TREATMENT

A brief description of the film idea. Usually, a writer needs an agent or a track record to generate interest in a treatment. Some producers feel that an outline differs from a treatment in that the outline is a scene-by-scene description of the film. Some screenwriters have sold their treatments with verbal pitches.

V VOICE OVER (V.O.)

Indicates we hear a voice but do not see the character speaking the line. The person is neither in the scene nor in the shot. This is different from OFF-SCREEN (O.S.) in which the speaker is off camera, but in the scene.

The voice track is superimposed on the shot. For example, a VOICE OVER could be over a telephone, answering machine or speaker. In some cases, the VOICE OVER is that of the character; he may not be seen on screen but he may be thinking out loud, reading a letter, or serving as the narrator. In directions, VOICE OVER or OFF STAGE should be spelled out in capital letters. Such as:

VOICE OVER the airport loudspeaker.

But, as a qualifier of a character name, use the abbreviation ("V.O.") in capital letters with periods. An example:

                    CAPT. THROCKMORTON (V.O.)
           . . . my dearest Ludvinnia,
          I'm writing this to you as
          we're about to go into
          battle . . .

If Capt. Throckmorton's voice came from an answering machine and Ludvinnia was listening to the machine, and then he appeared on screen and spoke, you would not need to use "(continuing)" because the voice over dialogue and the spoken dialogue are treated as separate and different elements. An example:

                    CAPT. THROCKMORTON (V.O.)
          We're through! It's finished!
          I'm never going to see you
          again!

Throckmorton leaps through the French doors, knocks over the tray of crepes Suzette, and lands on the hobby horse.

                    CAPT. THROCKMORTON
          . . . Liar! Liar! Pants on
          fire!

BOOK 2

PLAYWRITING

The elements of style for playwriting are not nearly as complicated as those for screenwriting. The format is straightforward and specific, so the easiest, quickest and best way to present the rules for playwriting is to show you sample pages from a play.

In film, the screenwriter is admonished not to put anything in dialogue that can be shown on the screen. In theater, the playwright wants to be heard and words are his tool. The format underscores that—dialogue takes over the whole page. The playwright's words are sacrosanct. They cannot—and must not—be changed without permission.

But, the playwright cannot put on the show alone and other talent must be considered, such as the director, actors, lighting and set designer, costumer, stage manager, and stagehands. These craftspeople cannot do their jobs unless they receive instructions, so there must be room on the page for their cues, too.

SAMPLE STAGE PLAY

FUNNY YOU SHOULD ASK

A Joke

In One Act

by T. T. Throckmorton

T. T. Throckmorton
5 Independence St.
Columbia, IA 50057
Tel: 213.555-1212
FAX: 213.555-1234

CAST OF CHARACTERS

Dr. Throckmorton, about 50, a veterinarian

Ludvinnia, about 45, a client

Tabby, about eight, an asset

- 0 -

The action throughout takes place
in the veterinarian's examining room.

- 0 -

Time: The present.

- 0 -

SYNOPSES OF SCENES

ACT I

Scene 1   Ludvinnia's summer
           cottage on Cape Cod,
           mid-morning of an
           early September day

Scene 2   The same, shortly
           thereafter

Scene 3   The same, on the
           porch, shortly there-
           after

A second act would appear as:

A C T II

Scene 1   The same, late that
           afternoon

Scene 2   The same, in the
           Family Room, that
           evening

I-1-1*

ACT I

Scene 1

TIME: The present. Late
             morning.

SCENE: The examining room of
             Dr. Throckmorton's
             veterinary hospital.
             The usual parapherna-
             lia—table, shelves,
             box of tissues—fills
             the room. A box of
             kitty treats is on a
             table. Entrance SR.

AT RISE: DR. THROCKMORTON is
             spraying disinfectant
             on the examining
             table and polishing
             it with a cloth.
             LUDVINNIA ENTERS
             holding a shoe box.
             He continues for a
             moment, then looks up
             and smiles at Her.

                    LUDVINNIA
            (A half-smile. Downcast)
Dr. Throckmorton, I called. I'm Ludvinnia.

                    THROCKMORTON
            (He drops the smile and goes on
            polishing for a bit.)
How we doing?

            (LUDVINNIA fidgets. THROCKMORTON
            puts down the spray bottle, and
            points to the shoe box.)
What have we here?

*One-act plays would carry only arabic numerals for page numbers.

                         LUDVINNIA
I'm doing fine, but I'm very worried about my
dear pet.
                    (She clutches the box hard to Her.)

                       THROCKMORTON
                    (Nods, speaks solicitously.)
Yes, of course. Shall we have a look?

                    (LUDVINNIA puts the box on the ex-
                    amining tale. She sees a box of
                    tissues on the counter, and helps
                    herself. She dries her eyes.
                    THROCKMORTON makes a move to remove
                    the rubber band, but LUDVINNIA
                    holds up a hand to stop Him. She
                    pets the box, then yanks off the
                    rubber band. She looks hard into
                    the vet's eyes as She removes the
                    top of the box.)

                       THROCKMORTON
                    (Gasps - covers His eyes.)
It's . . . It's . . . a parakeet!

                    (He stares into the box. A five
                    count)
I'm sorry to tell you, Ma'am, but your parakeet
looks . . . dead, I mean, really kaput.

                         LUDVINNIA
What!
                    (She grabs THROCKMORTON by His la-
                    pels, and shakes Him. He is thrown
                    backwards and forwards several
                    times.)
That can't be! I loved that pet like I was a
bird!

                       THROCKMORTON
                    (smoothing His jacket)
No question you did.

LUDVINNIA
(imploring)
You don't understand. He's got to be okay or
I'll be guilt-ridden the rest of my life! I for-
got to feed him when I got up this morning only
to find Him like this later. He can't be kaput.

THROCKMORTON
You want confirmation of my diagnosis? Okay.
(He goes to the entrance, opens the
door, and makes twitching sounds to
call a cat.)

TABBY
(ENTERS the room)
Meeoooooowwwww!
(THROCKMORTON taps the top of the
examining table. TABBY jumps atop
the table. He walks around the shoe
box. He looks in and sniffs.)
Meow . . .

THROCKMORTON
(Feeding Him a kitty treat.)
Good kitty!
(TABBY takes the treat, hops off
the table and EXITS through the
open door.)

THROCKMORTON
That confirms it, Ludvinnia.
(He hands Her the box of tissues)
Your parakeet is gone.

LUDVINNIA
(Jutting Her chin, trying to be
brave.)
I was hoping you wouldn't say that. I still have
payments to make on him. What do I owe you?

                    THROCKMORTON
I'm sure you understand, Ludvinnia, what with
the exorbitant malpractice insurance costs . . .

          (LUDVINNIA crosses Her arms, raises
          an eyebrow and stares at Him.)

   . . . rising, taxes and so on my fee is
$400.00.

                    LUDVINNIA
          (Covering the box and clutching it
          to Her.)
Would you be kind enough to itemize that for me
. . . without the violin music?

                    THROCKMORTON
          (Rubbing His hands on the cleaning
          cloth.)
Certainly. It's $30.00 for the office visit, and
$370.00 for the cat scan.

          (THE LIGHTS BLACK OUT)

          and

              FINAL CURTAIN

              (Third source address here)

PLAYWRITING ELEMENTS

C   CAST OF CHARACTERS PAGE

A list of all the characters in the play; this follows the title page.

At one time, the character's importance was listed in descending order. To keep actors' egos in check, the cast is now listed "in order of appearance." This means the characters are listed in the order in which they appear or speak as the play progresses. The list is centered and typed in all capital letters just below the line reading: "CAST OF CHARACTERS." Included is a very brief description, i.e., age and role or relationship to the other characters listed.

Use a dingbat of some sort (i.e., a zero centered between hanging hyphens, "- 0 -") to separate the character list from a brief explanation of where and when the action takes place. If the date of the action is important, use another dingbat and center the date. Another dingbat should separate the notice of copyright, if using one; this is placed in the lower left-hand corner. For a one-act play, this would appear at the bottom of the first page, separated from the dialogue with a short line of dashes.

For a one-act play, the cast of characters would appear on the first page, at the top right, under the title and playwright's name. See page 143.

CHARACTER CUE

C

Indicating the performer who is speaking or the description of his action. It is centered and typed in all capital letters.

Skip a space above the cue and single space to the dialogue line or personal direction; double-space to a house direction.

With the character's first entrance, a description as complete as possible should follow in the stage directions. For example:

```
             THROCKMORTON
        (He is about 50, dressed quite
        stylishly in white tie and tails,
        and carries a walking stick. He is
        outfitted with a huge knapsack.)
```

Single-space to the first line of dialogue. Single-space to personal direction:

```
        (angrily)
```

Double-space to a house direction:

```
SOUND OFFSTAGE: crashing glass
```

Double-space after a house direction to continue dialogue or personal direction. Double-space to another house direction.

In stage directions and descriptions, characters' names are typed in capital letters. In dialogue, characters' names are typed in upper and lower case letters. In stage directions only, pronouns (such as "He," "She," "They") are capitalized.

C   COVER

The script should be placed in a binder that comes with its own metal fasteners or with the prongs attached. Do not use the clamp-type fastener. Label the cover with the name of the play, typed in all capital letters, the number of acts, and the author's name. For example:

FUNNY YOU SHOULD ASK

A One-Act Play

by T. T. Throckmorton

DIALOGUE

D

All dialogue is single-spaced, typed in upper and lower case letters directly under the character name and runs across the page, up to 60 spaces, (or six inches) from margin to margin. If possible, avoid carrying a speech over to another page. If that happens, follow the character name on the next page with "(CONT'D)" to indicate it is an ongoing speech.

F

FIRST PAGE OF A SCENE

The first page of a scene is similar to the screenplay's slug line but it dispenses more detailed information, identifying the time, setting and action. The page will have the following information:

- The first page is paginated as such: "I-1-1" (for Act I, Scene 1, Page 1).

- One space under that, centered, is the act number, typed in all capital letters with a Roman numeral, such as: "ACT I."

- Skip a space. Center, underline and type, in upper and lower case letters, the scene number, such as "Scene 2."

- Then, you must identify "TIME:" "SCENE:" and "AT RISE:" The purpose of these three headlines is not only to present this information to the director and talent, but to enable the scenic designer, costumer, lighting designer, etc., to capture the author's vision. The protocol for these three headers is as follows:

  1. Skip a space after the scene number, and under that, in the middle of the page, in all capital letters type, "TIME:" (with a colon). Move five spaces and, in upper and lower case letters, type the time of the play (or scene); this could be the time of day, a day of the week, the season, year, or the elapsed time, such as "A half-hour later."

  2. Skip a space. Directly under "TIME:" type "SCENE:" Using the same margins you set for "TIME:" describe the scene when the curtain goes up, including relevant furniture, paintings, properties. Indicate the stage ENTRANCES.

  3. Skip a space. Directly under "SCENE:" type "AT RISE:" Keeping the same margins, describe the scene and action when the curtain goes up. If called for, indicate "SOUND:" such as rainfall; or "MUSIC:" (naming the piece, its source and intensity).

An example of the top of the first page:

I-1-1

ACT I

Scene 1

TIME:	Early morning, a Spring day.
SCENE:	The patio at LUDVINNIA'S cottage at Cape Cod.
AT RISE:	LUDVINNIA, dressed in tennis clothes, ENTERS carrying a tray.
	MUSIC (offstage) a Wagnerian Brunhilde in full voice for a ten count, then UNDER and FADE OUT.

                    LUDVINNIA
          (to the air)
Ah! How I love the sound and smell of thunder in
the morning!

M

MARGINS

- For dialogue, the margins should be 1-1/2" on the left and go to 1" on the right.

- The page number is placed about 1/2" from the top of the page (see PAGINATION, page 157).

- The bottom margin is about 1" but should be flexible, to allow for the most convenient place to end the page.

PAGINATION

P

Pagination for stage plays is found in the upper right-hand corner. Three numbers are used; they are hyphenated. They represent the Act Number-Scene Number-Page Number, respectively. Single page numbers are used in one-act plays, regardless of the number of scenes.

Begin every new scene on a new page.

S

SCRIPT LENGTH

A full-length stage play averages 120 pages. Some plays run shorter; a few may take two or three evenings to complete! In other words, there is no set length for a play. And, one-act plays can be any length the playwright deems necessary. (On average, they run about 40 pages.)

Competitions often call for ten-minute plays. These have a maximum of ten pages—their presentation, from start to finish, should take no more than ten minutes. There are sometimes calls for plays shorter than ten minutes. If this is the case, specifications are usually spelled out.

SEARCH AND REPLACE

S

The "Search and Replace" feature of most computer software is an invaluable tool; it can be adapted to the playwriting format. Here's how it works:

- Give each character in your play a symbol or a two-letter identification. (List the character and his symbol on a piece of paper and keep it near your computer.) Be sure not to use a word such as "is," "or."

- Instead of hitting the tab key to get to the spot for the character cue, type the character identification letters at the left-hand margin and press "Return" or "Enter." Let's say you've given the character "THROCKMORTON" the identification of "TH." Following that, you type his dialogue. It would look like this:

```
TH
Imagine how bright those African children
are! Even the young ones I met—eight, nine
years old—all speaking Swahili!
          (He smiles)
```

- When you're ready, scroll back to the start of your play and use the "Search and Replace" tool. Enter the identification of the character for the "Search" (including the return); and for "Replace." Enter the number of tabs you need to put the character cue in the correct place and type the character's full name in all capital letters. Then, let the computer do its work. An example:

The screen asks: "Search for:"

Type in the ID for THROCKMORTON, which is "TH."

It now reads: Search for: "TH(return)" The screen now asks: "Replace with:" Here, you enter the full character cue with the correct number of tabs so it reads:

Replace with: "(tab)(tab)(tab)THROCKMORTON(return).

continued on next page

S   **SEARCH AND REPLACE** *continued from previous page*

The "Return" will activate the procedure. Every "TH" will be replaced with the properly formatted name of "THROCKMORTON."

You can use this shortcut for the character cue in screenwriting, but a macro must be used to set the two right-hand margins (dialogue and edge of paper). Once you get the hang of the "Search and Replace" shortcut, it'll be like falling in love all over again.

STAGE DIRECTION

There are two types of stage direction: "personal" and "house."

Personal stage directions are aimed at the characters in the play and deal either with *action* or the *manner* in which a line is delivered. A direction pertaining to action will state what and/or how the character will do something. Enclose the direction in parentheses and place it 15 spaces from the left margin (let it run 35 spaces or so). An example:

```
              THROCKMORTON
          (crosses rapidly SL behind the
          sofa to the door)
```

A direction indicating manner suggests demeanor or emotion. The format is the same, for example:

```
              LUDVINNIA
          (quite distraught, near tears)
```

A stage direction may indicate both action and manner. An example:

```
              THROCKMORTON
          (leaps to His feet . . .
          angrily . . .)
```

Some personal stage directions are typed in all capital letters, such as "ENTER" and "EXIT" and all character names. Personal pronouns, such as he, she, they, are capitalized. An example:

```
              LUDVINNIA
          (ENTERS from the dining room)
My late husband was such a generous man. In
his will, he said I should spend thirty-
five-thousand-dollars on a stone. Do you
like it?
```

continued on next page

S

STAGE DIRECTION *continued from previous page*

```
                    (THROCKMORTON quickly crosses to
                    Her, takes Her hand, and looks at
                    the sparkler on Her finger. He
                    smiles at LUDVINNIA. He laughs as
                    He EXITS through the front door.)
          He can't say I took a lot for granite.
```

House stage directions are cues to anyone involved in the "behind-the-scenes" production of the play, i.e., those responsible for lighting, curtain, sound effects, music, offstage cues, or stagehands maneuvering props, sets, backdrops, etc. To emphasize these directions, the format calls for them to be placed in parentheses and typed in all capital letters. There should be a blank space above and below and the directions are indented 15 spaces. Included are cues for LIGHTING, MUSIC; SOUND; SPECIAL EFFECTS; OFFSTAGE cues or sounds.

Centered and underlined, but without parentheses, are: "END OF ACT 1"; "ACT ONE CURTAIN"; "FINAL CURTAIN."

SYNOPSES OF SCENES PAGE

This page follows the Cast of Characters page. It is not used for one-act plays. List all the scenes where the action takes place in the center of the page. You can compile this page easily by copying the scene description from the "SCENE:" headings that begin each scene.

T THE THEATER

You can perform a play in any kind of facility—two boards and a passion, the back of a wagon, a Proscenium Stage, Thrust Stage, Theater in the Round—but the first thing you need is a stage. The following diagram is a bird's-eye view of a Proscenium stage and its nine acting areas. Stage left and stage right are as they would be for an actor standing on stage facing the audience.

STAGEPLOT

. . . .

UPSTAGE

UP	UC	UL
upright	upcenter	upleft

. . . .

R	C	L
rightcenter	center	leftcenter

. . . .

DR	DC	DL
downright	downcenter	downleft

. . . .

DOWNSTAGE

. . . .

ORCHESTRA
(AUDIENCE)

TITLE PAGE

T

The first page of the script that carries the following specific information:

- The title of the play in all capital letters, centered on the page, about a third of the way down.

- The type of play it is (Drama, Comedy, Farce, etc.), centered beneath the title and typed one line down, in upper and lower case letters.

- The number of acts, centered beneath the genre and typed one line down, in upper and lower case letters. For example: "A One-Act Play" or "In Two Acts."

- The author's name, centered beneath the number of acts and typed one line down, in upper and lower case letters.

- The source address, in the lower right-hand corner (See Book 1, page 18.). This offers the author's (or agent's) name, complete address, telephone number, fax number, e-mail (if you wish).

GLOSSARY

AAR	Association of Authors Representatives 10 Astor Place, 3rd Floor New York, NY 10003 Tel: 212.353-3709
	For a list of agents with addresses and their canon of ethics, send a $7 check plus a self-addressed business envelope with correct postage.
Acting Area	The area of the stage or of a specific set where actors perform
Actor	A performer. Refers to both men and women
Acts	See Book 1, page 29
Ad Lib	See Book 1, page 31
Address	See Book 1, page 32
Adaptation	Indicating the written piece existed in another form and was (perhaps) originated by a different author
Agents	See AAR above. Also, see Book 1, page 33
Apron	The area of the stage in front of the main drape
Arena Theater	Any performance that takes place in a centered area surrounded by the audience
Aside	When the performer speaks directly to the audience
Audition	A tryout in front of the director, producer(s), playwright(s) or others for a role in the play. An audition call for acting and, sometimes, singing and/or dancing
Backer	The person who finances the show. Also called an "Angel."
Beat	A brief moment without dialogue. See Book 1, page 37
Blackout	Ending of a scene by the rapid dimming of the lights. A brief blackout may indicate the passage of time
Blocking	Diagrams indicating where and when the actors move, or the actual movements, action or placement of the actors. See Book 1, page 39.
Book	The play script. In a musical, the libretto is referred to as the book; the music and lyrics are referred to as the score
Break a Leg!	The common way, in the theater, of wishing someone good luck. (Theater superstition indicates you should say the opposite of what you mean.)
Cast	The actors performing in the play. The Cast of Characters lists the roles in a play.

Cue	An indication by word, action or sound that signals the next line or action. House cues are given to change sets, lights, props, sound effects, music.
Curtain	Raising the main curtain indicates the opening of a play or a scene dropping the main curtain indicates the end of a play or scene. When seen in a script, "CURTAIN" usually means to bring it down
Curtain(s)	Hanging drapery on stage. May be the main or house curtain
Curtain Call	Actors bowing at the end of a play.
Dim	To lower the intensity of the light onstage
Double casting	Casting the same actor for more than one role, either as a dramatic device or to reduce the number of actors needed to perform in that play
Downstage (DS)	The area towards the apron or the footlights—in the direction of the audience
Ellipsis marks	See Book 1, page 65
Enter/Exit	Personal direction: "ENTER" when a character comes on stage; "EXIT" when the character leaves. See Book 1, page 67
Equity	Actors union. Actors Equity Association or AEA
Face	To stand face-to-face or directly in front of another actor
Fade in/Fade out	The slow or gradual dimming of lights in or out
Fourth wall	The imaginary wall implied by the curtain line or the proscenium. The playwright's efficacy in "breaking through" the fourth wall depends on his craftsmanship in creating an illusion of reality that engages the audience
French Scene	The scene begins with the entrance of one or more significant characters and ends with the exit of one or more
Green Room	A place set aside for actors where they can wait between scenes—they'll be out of the way but easily found
Lead	The principal character. There may be more than one lead. This may also refer to the actor playing a role: the top banana
Lines	The speeches that make up the dialogue of a script
Macro	See Book 1, page 82
Offstage	Refers to the backstage area or somewhere NOT on stage. It also refers to any action or sound not seen onstage
Onstage	Within the acting area or playing space

Principals	The leading characters in a play
Producer	A backer. An individual or organization that provides the means to mount a production
Prompt Book or Script	The detailed notes of the play's action, kept by the stage manager
Properties, Props	The personal and set pieces necessary for the "business" of the play. Pictures and lamps are set props; handkerchiefs, handbags and canes are personal props
Property	The script
Proscenium	The frame surrounding the stage. The audience sees the play through the proscenium opening, or arch
SASE	A self-addressed, stamped envelope. See Book 1, page 110
Scrim	Known as theatrical gauze, this is a woven backdrop that may be transparent (when lit from behind) or opaque (when lit from the front). It is used for dramatic effect
Script length	A full-length play runs about 120 pages. A one-act play has no set length but generally runs no more than 40 pages. A ten-minute play has a maximum of ten pages.
Sides	Manuscript "sides" contain only the lines to be spoken by a specific character, preceded by three or four cue words
Stage center	The exact center of the playing area. May be UC, C, or, DC
Stage directions	Script indications for movement or action
Stage left	When facing the audience, this is the stage area to the left side of the actor. May be divided and designated as SL, UL, DL, DSL etc.
Stage Right	When facing the audience, this is the stage area to the right side of the actor. May be divided and designated SR, UR, DR, DR, etc.
Stand-in	A replacement for the actor, particularly for a dangerous, undesirable, or difficult bit of action.
Thrust Stage	Any stage space that extends into the audience
Upstage	The area away from the audience or toward the back of the stage. An actor "upstages" others when he moves into this area and draws attention to himself by enacting a sight gag not seen by the other actors or by forcing them to turn their backs on the audience
Wardrobe	All costumes and accessories for a play

REFERENCE WORKS

Here are suggestions for reference works a writer should have on a nearby shelf, or know how to speedily access on the computer:

- Dictionary: One can never have enough dictionaries, of all sizes, styles and types, such as Webster's, Columbia, Oxford, and so on.
- Webster's Dictionary of Synonyms and Antonyms
- Rodale's The Synonym Finder
- Roget's International Thesaurus
- March's Thesaurus-Dictionary
- Fowler's Modern English Usage
- Chicago Manual of Style
- New York Times Manual
- Bartlett's Familiar Quotations
- The World Almanac
- Information, Please
- World Atlas

LITERARY AGENTS

A

ABOVE THE LINE AGENCY
9200 Sunset Blvd., Suite 401
West Hollywood, CA 90069
Tel. 310-859-6115
Fax 310-859-6119

ACME TALENT & LITERARY
6310 San Vicente Blvd., Suite 520
Los Angeles, CA 90048
Tel. 213-954-2263, 212-328-0388
Fax 213-954-2262-212-328-0391
e-mail: adamlieb@aol.com

THE AGENCY
1800 Avenue of The Stars, Suite 400
Los Angeles, CA 90067
Tel. 310-551-3000
Fax 310-551-1424

**AGENCY FOR THE PERFORMING
ARTS INC. (LA)**
9000 Sunset Blvd., Suite 1200
Los Angeles, CA 90069
Tel. 310-273-0744
Fax 310-888-4242

**AGENCY FOR THE PERFORMING
ARTS INC. (NY)**
888 Seventh Avenue
New York, NY 10100
Tel. 212-582-1500
Fax 212-245-1647

ALPERN GROUP
4400 Coldwater Canyon, Suite 125
Studio City, CA 91604
Tel. 818-752-1877
Fax 818-752-1859

AMBROSIO/MORTIMER & ASSOC. (LA)
5750 Wilshire Blvd., Suite 512
Los Angeles, CA 90036
Tel. 213-954-1888

AMBROSIO/MORTIMER & ASSOC. (NY)
165 West 46th Street, Suite 1214
New York, NY 10036
Tel. 212-719-1677
Fax 212-768-9361

AMSEL EISENSTADT & FRAZIER INC.
6310 San Vicente Blvd., Suite 401
Los Angeles, CA 90048
Tel. 213-939-1188
Fax 213-939-0630

ANNETTE VAN DUREN AGENCY
925 North Sweetzer Avenue, Suite 12
Los Angeles, CA 90069
Tel. 213-650-3643
Fax 213-654-3893

ARTHUR B. GREENE
101 Park Avenue, 43rd Floor
New York, NY 10178
Tel. 212-661-8200
Fax 212-370-7884

THE ARTISTS AGENCY
230 West 55th Street, Suite 29D
New York, NY 10019
Tel. 212-245-6960
Fax 212-333-7420

THE ARTISTS AGENCY
10000 Santa Monica Blvd., Suite 305
Los Angeles, CA 90067
Tel. 310-277-7779
Fax 310-785-9338

THE ARTISTS GROUP (LA)
10100 Santa Monica Blvd., Suite 2490
Los Angeles, CA 90067-4115
Tel. 310-552-1100, 212-536-1452
Fax 310-277-9513

B

THE BARRY PERELMAN AGENCY
9200 Sunset Blvd., Suite 1201
Los Angeles, CA 90069
Tel. 310-274-5999

BECSEY/WISDOM/KALAJIAN
9229 Sunset Blvd., Suite 710
Los Angeles, CA 90069
Tel. 310-550-0535
e-mail: becsey@aol.com

THE BENNETT AGENCY
150 South Barrington Avenue, Suite 1
Los Angeles, CA 90049
Tel. 310-471-2251
Fax 310-471-2254

BERZON TALENT AGENCY
336 East 17th Street
Costa Mesa, CA 92627
Tel. 714-631-5936, 818-548-1565
Fax 714-631-6881-818-548-1560
http://www.berzon.com

THE BOHRMAN AGENCY
8489 West Third Street
Los Angeles, CA 90048
Tel. 213-653-6701
Fax 213-653-6702

THE BRANDT COMPANY
15250 Ventura Blvd., Suite 720
Sherman Oaks, CA 91403
Tel. 818-783-7747
Fax 818-784-6012
e-mail: brandtco@aol.com

BRESLER-KELLY & ASSOCIATES
15760 Ventura Blvd., Suite 1730
Encino, CA 91436
Tel. 818-905-1155

BRET ADAMS, LTD.
448 West 44th Street
New York, NY 10036
Tel. 212-265-2212
e-mail: badamsltd@aol.com

**BRODER-KURLAND-WEBB-
UFFNER AGENCY**
9242 Beverly Blvd., Suite 200
Beverly Hills, CA 90210
Tel. 310-281-3400, 310-281-3434
Fax 310-276-3207

BRUCE BROWN AGENCY
1033 Gayley Avenue, Suite 207
Los Angeles, CA 90024
Tel. 310-208-1835
Fax 310-208-2485

C

THE CALLAMARO LITERARY AGENCY
427 North Canon Drive, Suite 202
Beverly Hills, CA 90210
Tel. 310-274-6783
Fax 310-274-6536

CANDACE LAKE AGENCY
9229 Sunset Blvd., Suite 320
Los Angeles, CA 90069
Tel. 310-247-2115
Fax 310-247-2116

CHASIN AGENCY
8899 Beverly Blvd., Suite 716
Los Angeles, CA 90048
Tel. 310-278-7505
Fax 310-275-6685

CINEMA TALENT AGENCY
8033 Sunset Blvd., Suite 808
West Hollywood, CA 90046
Tel. 213-656-1937
Fax 213-654-4678

CIRCLE OF CONFUSION LTD.
666 5th Avenue, Suite 303G
New York, NY 10103
Tel. 212-969-0653
Fax 212-975-7748
e-mail: circleltd@aol.com

CNA & ASSOCIATES
1925 Century Park E., Suite 750
Los Angeles, CA 90067
Tel. 310-556-4343
Fax 310-556-4633

THE COPPAGE COMPANY
11501 Chandler Blvd.
North Hollywood, CA 91601
Tel. 818-980-1106
Fax 818-509-1474
e-mail: coppage@aol.com

CREATIVE ARTISTS AGENCY
9830 Wilshire Blvd.
Beverly Hills, CA 90212
Tel. 310-288-4545

CURTIS BROWN LTD. (NY)
10 Astor Place
New York, NY 10003
Tel. 212-473-5400

D

DADE/SCHULTZ ASSOCIATES
12302 Sarah Street
Studio City, CA 91604
Tel. 818-760-3100
Fax 818-760-1395

THE DANIEL OSTROFF AGENCY
9200 Sunset Blvd., Suite 402
Los Angeles, CA 90069
Tel. 310-278-2020
Fax 310-278-4369

DAVID SHAPIRA & ASSOCIATES
15301 Ventura Blvd., Suite 345
Sherman Oaks, CA 91403
Tel. 818-906-0322
Fax 818-783-2562

DON BUCHWALD & ASSOC. INC.
6500 Wilshire Blvd., 22nd Floor
Los Angeles, CA 90048
Tel. 213-655-7400
Fax 213-655-7470

DON BUCHWALD & ASSOC. INC.
10 East 44th Street
New York, NY 10017
Tel. 212-867-1200

DOUROUX & CO.
445 South Beverly Drive, Suite 310
Beverly Hills, CA 90212-4401
Tel. 310-552-0900
Fax 310-552-0920

DYTMAN & ASSOCIATES
9200 Sunset Blvd., Suite 809
Los Angeles, CA 90069
Tel. 310-274-8844
Fax 310-274-7448

E

ELAINE MARKSON LIT. AGENCY
44 Greenwich Avenue
New York, NY 10011
Tel. 212-243-8480
Fax 212-691-9014

ENDEAVOR
9701 Wilshire Blvd., 10th Floor
Beverly Hills, CA 90212
Tel. 310-248-2000, 310-248-2020
Fax 310-226-8511

EPSTEIN-WYCKOFF & ASSOC. (LA)
280 South Beverly Drive, Suite 400
Beverly Hills, CA 90212
Tel. 310-278-7222
Fax 310-278-4640

EPSTEIN-WYCKOFF & ASSOC. (NY)
311 West 43rd Street, Suite 304
New York, NY 10036
Tel. 212-586-9110
Fax 212-586-8019

F

FAVORED ARTISTS
122 South Robertson, Suite 202
Los Angeles, CA 90048
Tel. 310-247-1040
Fax 310-247-1048

THE FIELD-CECH AGENCY INC.
12725 Ventura Blvd., Suite D
Studio City, CA 91604
Tel. 818-980-2001
Fax 818-980-0754

FILM ARTISTS ASSOCIATES
13563 Ventura Blvd., 2nd Floor
Sherman Oaks, CA 91403
Tel. 818-386-9669
Fax 818-386-9363

FLORA ROBERTS INC.
157 West 57th Street
New York, NY 10019
Tel. 212-355-4165

G

THE GAGE GROUP, INC. (LA)
9255 Sunset Blvd., Suite 515
Los Angeles, CA 90069
Tel. 310-859-8777

THE GAGE GROUP, INC. (NY)
315 West 57th Street, Suite 4H
New York, NY 10019
Tel. 212-541-5250
Fax 212-956-7466
e-mail: gageny@aol.com

GEORGES BORCHARDT INC.
136 East 57th Street
New York, NY 10022
Tel. 212-753-5785
Fax 212-838-6518

THE GERSH AGENCY (LA)
232 North Canon Drive
Beverly Hills, CA 90210
Tel. 310-274-6611
Fax 310-274-3923 / 310-274-4035

THE GERSH AGENCY (NY)
130 West 42nd Street, 24th Floor
New York, NY 10036
Tel. 212-997-1818
Fax 212-391-8459/212-997-1978
e-mail: gershny@aol.com

GOLD/MARSHAK/LIEDTKE AGENCY
3500 West Olive Avenue, Suite 1400
Burbank, CA 91505
Tel. 818-972-4300
Fax 818-955-6411

H

**H.W.A. TALENT
REPRESENTATIVES (NY)**
36 East 22nd Street, 3rd Floor
New York, NY 10010
Tel. 212-529-4555

HAROLD MATSON CO.
276 Fifth Avenue
New York, NY 10001
Tel. 212-679-4490
Fax 212-545-1224

HAROLD R. GREENE INC.
13900 Marquesas Way, #C-Suite 83
Marina del Rey, CA 90292
Tel. 310-823-5393

HENDERSON-HOGAN (LA)
247 South Beverly Drive, Suite 102
Beverly Hills, CA 90212
Tel. 310-274-7815
Fax 310-274-0751

HENDERSON-HOGAN (NY)
850 Seventh Avenue, Suite1003
New York, NY 10019
Tel. 212-765-5190
Fax 212-586-2855

HOHMAN, MAYBANK & LIEB
9229 Sunset Blvd., Suite 700
Los Angeles, CA 90069
Tel. 310-274-4600
Fax 310-274-4741

I

INNOVATIVE ARTISTS (LA)
1999 Avenue of The Stars, Suite 2850
Los Angeles, CA 90067
Tel. 310-553-5200
Fax 310-557-2211

INNOVATIVE ARTISTS (NY)
141 Fifth Avenue, Suite 3-South
New York, NY 10010
Tel. 212-253-6900
Fax 212-253-1198

IRV SCHECHTER CO.
9300 Wilshire Blvd., Suite 400
Beverly Hills, CA 90212
Tel. 310-278-8070
Fax 310-278-6058

J

J. MICHAEL BLOOM & ASSOCIATES
9255 Sunset Blvd., Suite 710
Los Angeles, CA 90069
Tel. 310-275-6800
Fax 310-275-6941

**THE JACK SCAGNETTI TALENT &
LITERARY AGENCY**
5118 Vineland, Suite 102
North Hollywood, CA 91601
Tel. 818-762-3871, 818-761-0580

JANKLOW & NESBIT ASSOCIATES
598 Madison Avenue
New York, NY 10022
Tel. 212-421-1700
Fax 212-980-3671
e-mail: postmaster@janklow.com

JEROME SIEGEL ASSOCIATES INC.
1680 North Vine, Suite 617
Hollywood, CA 90028
Tel. 213-466-0185

JIM PREMINGER AGENCY
1650 Westwood Blvd., Suite 201
Los Angeles, CA 90024-5613
Tel. 310-475-9491, 310-470-2934
e-mail: e-mail: rls@loop.com

THE JON KLANE AGENCY
120 El Camino Drive, Suite 112
Beverly Hills, CA 90212
Tel. 310-278-0178
Fax 310-278-0179

K

**THE KAPLAN-STAHLER-GUMER
AGENCY**
8383 Wilshire Blvd., Suite 923
Beverly Hills, CA 90211-2408
Tel. 213-653-4483
e-mail: ksagency@aol.com

KEN SHERMAN & ASSOCIATES
9507 Santa Monica Blvd., Suite 211
Beverly Hills, CA 90210
Tel. 310-273-8840

L

THE LANTZ OFFICE
888 Seventh Avenue, 25th Floor
New York, NY 10106
Tel. 212-586-0200
Fax 212-262-6659

LARRY GROSSMAN & ASSOC.INC.
211 South Beverly Drive, Suite 206
Beverly Hills, CA 90212
Fax 310-550-8129
President/Literary: Larry Grossman

LENHOFF & LENHOFF
9200 Sunset Blvd., Suite 1026
Los Angeles, CA 90069
Tel. 310-550-3900
Fax 310-550-3983

LESLIE B. KALLEN LITERARY AGENCY
15303 Ventura Blvd., Suite 900
Sherman Oaks, CA 91403
Tel. 818-906-2785
Fax 818-906-8931

LINDA SIEFERT & ASSOCIATES
8A Brunswick Gardens
London, W8 4AJ England
Tel. 44/171-229-5163

M

MAJOR CLIENTS AGENCY
345 North Maple Drive, Suite 395
Beverly Hills, CA 90210
Tel. 310-205-5000
Fax 310-205-5099

THE MARION ROSENBERG OFFICE
8428 Melrose Place, Suite B
Los Angeles, CA 90069
Tel. 213-653-7383
Fax 213-653-9268

MARTIN HURWITZ ASSOCIATES
427 North Canon Drive, Suite 215
Beverly Hills, CA 90210
Tel. 310-2740240

MEDIA ARTISTS GROUP
8383 Wilshire Blvd., Suite 954
Beverly Hills, CA 90211
Tel. 213-658-5050
Fax 213-658-7871

METROPOLITAN TALENT AGENCY
4526 Wilshire Blvd.
Los Angeles, CA 90010
Tel. 213-857-4500
Fax 213-857-4599

MICHAEL D. ROBINS & ASSOCIATES
15301 Ventura Blvd., Suite 412
Sherman Oaks, CA 91403
Tel. 818-343-1755
Fax 818-343-7355
e-mail: mdr2@msn.com

MIRISCH AGENCY
10100 Santa Monica Blvd., Suite 700
Los Angeles, CA 90067
Tel. 310-282-9940
Fax 310-282-0702

MITCHELL J. HAMILBURG AGENCY
292 South La Cienega Blvd., Suite 312
Beverly Hills, CA 90211
Tel. 310-657-1501
Fax 310-657-4968

MONTEIRO-ROSE AGENCY INC.
17514 Ventura Blvd., Suite 205
Encino, CA 91316
Tel. 818-501-1177
Fax 818-501-1194

O

ORIGINAL ARTISTS
417 South Beverly Drive, Suite 201
Beverly Hills, CA 90212
Tel. 310-277-1251
Fax 310-553-7448

P

**PARADIGM TALENT AND
LITERARY AGENCY (LA)**
10100 Santa Monica Blvd., 25th Floor
Los Angeles, CA 90067
Tel. 310-277-4400
Fax 310-277-7820

PARTOS COMPANY
6363 Wilshire Blvd., Suite 227
Los Angeles, CA 90048
Tel 213-876-5500
213-876-7836
e-mail partos@partos.com

PAUL KOHNER INC.
9300 Wilshire Blvd., Suite 555
Beverly Hills, CA 90212
Tel. 310-550-1060
Fax 310-276-1083

PETER TURNER AGENCY
3000 West Olympic Blvd., Suite 1438
Santa Monica, CA 90404
Tel. 310-315-4772

PHOENIX LITERARY AGENCY
315 South F Street
Livingston, Montana 59047
Tel. 406-222-2848

**THE PLESHETTE-MILNER
LITERARY AGENCY**
2700 North Beachwood Drive
Los Angeles, CA 90068
Tel. 213-465-0428

PREFERRED ARTISTS
16633 Ventura Blvd., Suite 1421
Encino, CA 91436
Tel. 818-990-2736

PREMIERE ARTISTS AGENCY
8899 Beverly Blvd., Suite 510
Los Angeles, CA 90048
Tel. 310-271-1414
Fax 310-205-3981

R

REECE HALSEY AGENCY
8733 Sunset Blvd., Suite 101
Los Angeles, CA 90069
Tel. 310-652-2409, 415-789-9191
Fax 310-652-7595
98 Main St.-No. 704
Tiburon-CA 94920

RENAISSANCE LITERARY AGENCY
9220 Sunset Blvd., Suite 302
Los Angeles, CA 90069
Tel. 310-858-5365
Fax 310-858-5389

THE RICHARD HERMAN AGENCY
124 Lasky Drive, 2nd Floor
Beverly Hills, CA 90212
Tel. 310-550-8913
Fax 310-550-0259

RICHARD PARKS AGENCY
138 East 16th Street, Suite 5-B
New York, NY 10003
Tel. 212-254-9067

THE RICHLAND AGENCY
11777 San Vicente Blvd., Suite 702
Los Angeles, CA 90049
Tel. 310-571-1833
Fax 310-571-1844

ROSENSTONE/WENDER
3 E 48th Street
New York, NY 10017
Tel. 212-832-8330
Fax 212-759-4524

ROSLYN TARG LITERARY AGENCY
105 West 13th Street, Suite 15-E
New York, NY 10011
Tel. 212-206-9390
Fax 212-989-6233
e-mail: roslyntarg@aol.com

THE ROTHMAN AGENCY
9401 Wilshire Blvd., Suite 830
Beverly Hills, CA 90212
Tel. 310-247-9898
Fax 310-247-9888

S

SANDRA WATT LITERARY AGENCY
8033 Sunset Blvd., Suite 4053
Hollywood, CA 90046
Tel. 213-851-1021

THE SANFORD-GROSS AGENCY
1015 Gayley Avenue, Suite 301
Los Angeles, CA 90024
Tel. 310-208-2100
Fax 310-208-6704
e-mail: sgagency@aol.com

THE SARNOFF CO. INC.
10 Universal City Plaza, Suite 2000
Universal City, CA 91608
Tel. 818-754-3708

SCHIOWITZ/CLAY/ROSE INC.
1680 North Vine Street, Suite 614
Los Angeles, CA 90028
Tel. 213-463-7300

SHAPIRO-LICHTMAN INC.
8827 Beverly Blvd.
Los Angeles, CA 90048
Tel. 310-859-8877
Fax 310-859-7153

**SMITH-GOSNELL-NICHOLSON
& ASSOCIATES**
1515 Palisades Drive
P.O. Box 1166
Pacific Palisades, CA 90272
Tel. 310-459-0307
Fax 310-4547987

**SOLOWAY, GRANT, KOPALOFF
& ASSOCIATES**
6399 Wilshire Blvd.
Los Angeles, CA 90048
Tel. 213-782-1854
Fax 213-782-1877

STEPHANIE MANN AGENCY
880 25th Avenue, Suite 302
San Francisco, CA 94121
Tel. 415-750-1827
Fax 415-750-1837

STEPHANIE ROGERS & ASSOCIATES
3575 Cahuenga Blvd. West, 2nd Floor
Los Angeles, CA 90068
Tel. 213-851-5155

STERLING LORD LITERISTIC INC.
65 Bleecker Street
New York, NY 10012
Tel. 212-780-6050
Fax 212-780-6095

STONE MANNERS AGENCY
8091 Selma Avenue
Los Angeles, CA 90046
Tel. 213-654-7575

**SUSAN SCHULMAN
LITERARY AGENCY**
454 West 44th Street
New York, NY 10036-5203
Tel. 212-713-1633
Fax 212-581-8830
e-mail: schulman@aol.com

SUSAN SMITH & ASSOCIATES
121 North San Vicente Blvd.
Beverly Hills, CA 90211
Tel. 213-852-4777
Fax 213-658-7170

T

THE TANTLEFF OFFICE
375 Greenwich Street, Suite 700
New York, NY 10013
Tel. 212-941-3939
Fax 212-941-3948

THE TURTLE AGENCY
12456 Ventura Blvd., Suite 1
Studio City, CA 91604-2406
Tel. 818-506-6898
Fax 818-506-1723
e-mail: cturtlewal@aol.com

TWENTIETH CENTURY ARTISTS
15315 Magnolia Blvd., Suite 429
Sherman Oaks, CA 91403
Tel. 818-788-5516

U - V

UNITED TALENT AGENCY
9560 Wilshire Blvd., Suite 500
Beverly Hills, CA 90212
Tel. 310-273-6700
Fax 310-247-1111

VISION ART MANAGEMENT
9200 Sunset Blvd., Penthouse One
Los Angeles, CA 90069-3502
Tel. 310-888-3288
Fax 310-888-2268

W

THE WALLERSTEIN COMPANY INC.
6399 Wilshire Blvd., Suite 914
Los Angeles, Ca 90048
Tel. 213-782-0225
Fax 213-782-0381
e-mail: msagent@aol.com

WARDEN WHITE & ASSOCIATES
8444 Wilshire Blvd., 4th Floor
Beverly Hills, CA 90211
Tel. 213-852-1028

WILLIAM CARROLL AGENCY
139 North San Fernando Blvd., Suite A
Burbank, CA 91502
Tel. 818-848-9948
Fax 818-845-1769

WILLIAM MORRIS AGENCY (LA)
151 El Camino Drive
Beverly Hills, CA 90212
Tel. 310-859-4000
Fax 310-859-4462

WILLIAM MORRIS AGENCY (NY)
1325 Avenue of the Americas
New York, NY 10019
Tel. 212-586-5100
Fax 212-246-3583

WRIGHT CONCEPT
1811 W. Burbank Blvd., Suite 201
Burbank, CA 91506
Tel. 818-954-8943

WRITERS & ARTISTS AGENCY (LA)
924 Westwood Blvd., Suite 900
Los Angeles, CA 90024
Tel. 310-824-6300
Fax 310-824-6343

WRITERS & ARTISTS AGENCY (NY)
19 W. 44th St., Suite 1000
New York, Ny 10036
Tel. 212-391-1112/212-575-6397
Fax 212-398-9877/212-575-6397

LITERARY MANAGERS

3 ARTS ENTERTAINMENT INC.
9460 Wilshire Blvd., 7th Floor
Beverly Hills, CA 90212
Tel. 310-888-3200, 212-262-6565
Fax 310-888-3210, 212-246-1522

ADDIS-WECHSLER & ASSOCIATES
955 South Carrillo Drive, Suite 300
Los Angeles, CA 90048
Tel. 310-954-9000
Fax 213-954-9009

BRILLSTEIN-GREY ENTERTAINMENT
9150 Wilshire Blvd., Suite 350
Beverly Hills, CA 90212
Tel. 310-275-6135
Fax 310-275-6180

BROWN GROUP
9300 Wilshire Blvd., Suite 508
Beverly Hills, CA 90212
Tel. 310-247-2755
Fax 310-247-2758

CARLYLE PRODUCTIONS & MANAGEMENT
639 North Larchmont, Suite 207
Los Angeles, CA 90004
Tel. 213-848-4960
Fax 213-469-9558
e-mail: Carlyle@earthlink.net

DAVID ROTMAN PRODUCTIONS
1401 Ocean Ave., Suite 201
Santa Monica, CA 90405
Tel. 310-319-9500
Fax 310-576-1807

THE DRAIZIN COMPANY
500 South Buena Vista Street
Burbank, CA 91521-7280
Tel. 818-972-4756
Fax 818-972-4765

GOLD/MILLER COMPANY
9220 Sunset Blvd., Suite 320
Los Angeles, CA 90069
Tel. 310-278-8990
Fax 310-278-0288

HOFFLUND/POLONE
9615 Brighton Way, Suite 320
Beverly Hills, CA 90210
Tel. 310-859-1971
Fax 310-859-7250

HYLER MANAGEMENT
25 Sea Colony Drive
Santa Monica, CA 90405
Tel. 310-396-7811
Fax 310-392-8264

KEN GROSS MANAGEMENT
10345 West Olmpic Blvd., 3rd Floor
Los Angeles, CA 90064
Tel. 310-552-8480
Fax 310-229-9282

KROST/CHAPIN
9911 West Plco Blvd., PH 1
Los Angeles, CA 90035
Tel. 310-553-2203
Fax 310-553-0809
e-mail: kcprods@lainet.com

LASHER, MCMANUS & ROBINSON
2372 Veteran Ave., Suite 102
Los Angeles, CA 90064
Tel. 310-446-1466
Fax 310-446-1566

MELINDA JASON COMPANY
216 South Carmelina Avenue
Los Angeles, CA 90049
Tel. 310-472-8309
Fax 310-550-8839

RADMIN COMPANY
9201 Wilshire Blvd., Suite 305
Beverly Hills, CA 90210
Tel. 310-274-9515
Fax 310-274-0739

REVOLUTION PICTURES
275 South Beverly Drive, Suite 200
Beverly Hills, CA 90212
Tel. 310-288-0303
Fax 310-288-0404

SEVEN SUMMITS PICTURES & MANAGEMENT
8447 Wilshire Blvd., Suite 206
Beverly Hills, CA 90211
Tel. 213-655-0101
Fax. 213-655-2204

TAVEL/GROSS ENTERTAINMENT
9171 Wilshire Blvd., Suite 405
Beverly Hills, CA 90210
Tel. 310-278-6700
Fax 310-278-6770

VIVIANO ENTERTAINMENT
9107 Wilshire Blvd., Suite 500
Beverly Hills, CA 90210
Tel. 310-247-1221
Fax. 310-247-5734
e-mail: bviviano@aol.com

ZIDE MANAGEMENT
9100 Wilshire Blvd., Suite 615E
Beverly Hills, CA 90212
Tel. 310-887-2999
Fax. 310-887-2995
e-mail: zidefilms@directnet.com

ABOUT THE AUTHOR

PAUL ARGENTINI is a screenwriter, playwright, novelist and freelance writer. Awarded a Playwriting Fellowship by the Massachusetts Artists Foundation, he is a former Boston and Washington, D.C. editor, reporter and photographer. He is a graduate of Boston University. Paul resides in Great Barrington in the Berkshire Hills of western Massachusetts.